Table of Contents

Fractions

Decimals

Introduction
Review ①

Name _____ Date ___ / ___ / ___

Score ___ / 7

1 Write > (greater than), < (less than), or = (equal to) to compare the fractions.

(1) $\frac{2}{3}$ $\boxed{>}$ $\frac{1}{3}$

(2) $\frac{2}{4}$ $\boxed{<}$ $\frac{3}{4}$

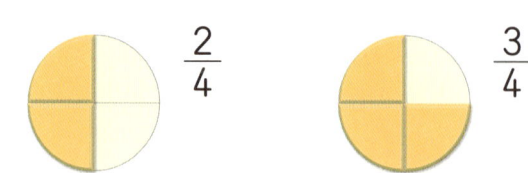

(3) 1 $\boxed{=}$ $\frac{2}{2}$

2 Write > (greater than), < (less than), or = (equal to) to compare the fractions.

(1) $\frac{4}{5}$ $\boxed{}$ $\frac{2}{5}$

(2) $\frac{2}{6}$ $\boxed{}$ $\frac{3}{6}$

(3) $\frac{5}{7}$ $\boxed{}$ $\frac{4}{7}$

(4) $\frac{8}{8}$ $\boxed{}$ 1

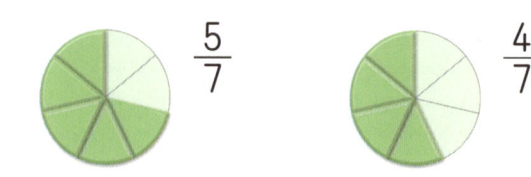
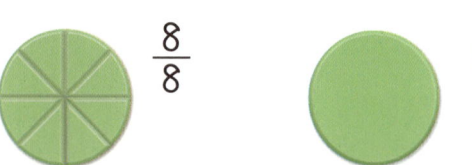

2

2 Introduction
Review ②

Fractions

- Proper Fraction: $\frac{1}{3}$, $\frac{2}{3}$, $\frac{3}{4}$ ·········· The numerator is smaller than the denominator.

- Improper Fraction: $\frac{3}{3}$, $\frac{4}{3}$, $\frac{9}{5}$ ·········· The numerator is equal to or larger than the denominator.

- Mixed Number: $1\frac{1}{3}$, $2\frac{2}{7}$ ·········· Whole Number + Proper Fraction

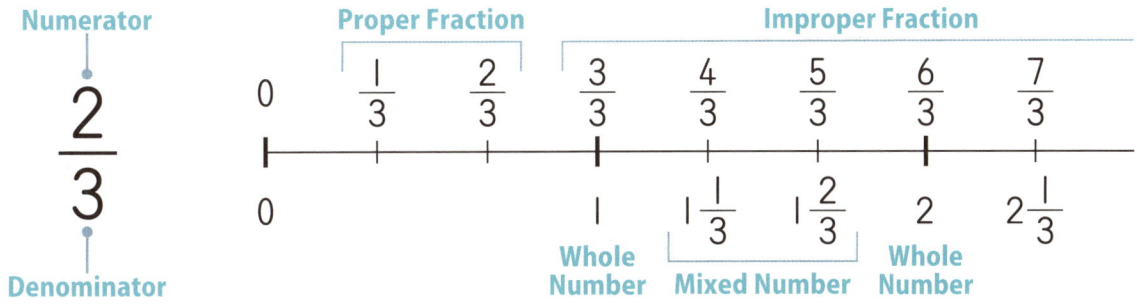

Numerator

$\frac{2}{3}$

Denominator

Proper Fraction

Improper Fraction

$\frac{1}{3}$ $\frac{2}{3}$ $\frac{3}{3}$ $\frac{4}{3}$ $\frac{5}{3}$ $\frac{6}{3}$ $\frac{7}{3}$

0

0   1 $1\frac{1}{3}$ $1\frac{2}{3}$ 2 $2\frac{1}{3}$

Whole Number   Mixed Number   Whole Number

---

1 Convert the improper fraction to a mixed number or a whole number.

(1) $\frac{11}{4}$ = $2\frac{3}{4}$

(2) $\frac{15}{5}$ = $\boxed{3}$

(3) $\frac{13}{6}$ = $\boxed{}\dfrac{\boxed{}}{\boxed{}}$

(4) $\frac{21}{7}$ = $\boxed{}$

Addition
Proper Fractions
Part One ①

1 Add.

(1) $\dfrac{1}{5} + \dfrac{1}{5} = \dfrac{2}{5}$

Just add the numerators.
Leave the denominators as they are.

(2) $\dfrac{1}{4} + \dfrac{2}{4} = \dfrac{\square}{4}$

(4) $\dfrac{3}{6} + \dfrac{2}{6} = \dfrac{\square}{\square}$

(3) $\dfrac{1}{3} + \dfrac{1}{3} = \dfrac{\square}{\square}$

(5) $\dfrac{2}{7} + \dfrac{1}{7} = \dfrac{\square}{\square}$

2 Add.

(1) $\dfrac{1}{5} + \dfrac{2}{5} =$

(3) $\dfrac{3}{7} + \dfrac{3}{7} =$

(2) $\dfrac{2}{6} + \dfrac{3}{6} =$

(4) $\dfrac{4}{8} + \dfrac{1}{8} =$

3 Stephanie biked $\dfrac{1}{3}$ of a mile to the store. She biked $\dfrac{1}{3}$ of a mile back home. How far did she bike in total?

$\dfrac{1}{3} + \dfrac{1}{3} = \dfrac{\square}{\square}$

Ans. _____ of a mile

4

Name

Date

/   /

Score

/ 9

1 Add.

(1) $\dfrac{2}{4} + \dfrac{1}{4} = \dfrac{\boxed{}}{\boxed{}}$

(3) $\dfrac{1}{8} + \dfrac{2}{8} = \dfrac{\boxed{}}{\boxed{}}$

(2) $\dfrac{3}{7} + \dfrac{2}{7} = \dfrac{\boxed{}}{\boxed{}}$

(4) $\dfrac{4}{9} + \dfrac{1}{9} = \dfrac{\boxed{}}{\boxed{}}$

2 Add.

(1) $\dfrac{4}{6} + \dfrac{1}{6} =$

(3) $\dfrac{2}{10} + \dfrac{5}{10} =$

(2) $\dfrac{2}{9} + \dfrac{2}{9} =$

(4) $\dfrac{3}{7} + \dfrac{3}{7} =$

3 Andrew is painting his room. He uses $\dfrac{3}{7}$ of the can of paint for the first coat and $\dfrac{1}{7}$ of the can of paint for the second coat. How much of the can of paint did he use?

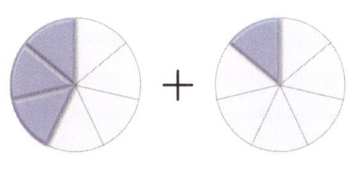

Ans. _____ of the can of paint

Check your answers.
If you missed any
problems, pick one
to retry.

5

5

Addition
Proper Fractions
Part One ③

Name

Date
/ /

Score
/ 9

1 Add.

(1) $\dfrac{2}{5} + \dfrac{2}{5} =$

(2) $\dfrac{3}{8} + \dfrac{4}{8} =$

(3) $\dfrac{4}{10} + \dfrac{3}{10} =$

(4) $\dfrac{5}{9} + \dfrac{2}{9} =$

(5) $\dfrac{1}{7} + \dfrac{3}{7} =$

(6) $\dfrac{3}{5} + \dfrac{1}{5} =$

(7) $\dfrac{4}{10} + \dfrac{5}{10} =$

(8) $\dfrac{4}{9} + \dfrac{4}{9} =$

2 Sam has $\dfrac{2}{5}$ of a liter of apple juice and $\dfrac{1}{5}$ of a liter of orange juice in his refrigerator. How much juice does he have in total?

Ans. _____ of a liter of juice

Check & Fix Check your answers. If you missed any problems, pick one to retry.

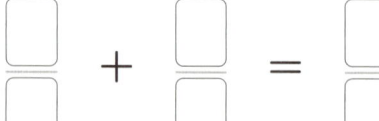

6

Addition
Proper Fractions
Part Two ①

Name

Date / /

Score / 6

1 Add.

$$\frac{2}{5} + \frac{4}{5} = \frac{6}{5}$$

> When the answer is an improper fraction, convert it to a mixed number or a whole number.
>
> $$\frac{6}{5} = \frac{5}{5} + \frac{1}{5} = 1 + \frac{1}{5}$$

$$= 1\frac{1}{5}$$

2 Add.

(1) $$\frac{2}{4} + \frac{3}{4} = \frac{5}{4}$$

$$= \boxed{}\frac{\boxed{}}{\boxed{}}$$

(2) $$\frac{2}{3} + \frac{3}{3} = \frac{\boxed{}}{\boxed{}}$$

$$=$$

(3) $$\frac{2}{6} + \frac{5}{6} =$$

(4) $$\frac{4}{7} + \frac{5}{7} =$$

3 Jack has $\frac{2}{3}$ of a yard of green fabric and $\frac{2}{3}$ of a yard of blue fabric. How many yards of fabric does he have altogether?

Ans. _____ yards

Addition
Proper Fractions
Part Two ②

Name

Date   /   /

Score   / 7

1 Add.

(1) $\dfrac{5}{7} + \dfrac{3}{7} = \dfrac{\boxed{}}{\boxed{}}$

=

(2) $\dfrac{2}{6} + \dfrac{4}{6} = \dfrac{\boxed{}}{\boxed{}}$

= |

2 Add.

(1) $\dfrac{3}{5} + \dfrac{4}{5} =$

(3) $\dfrac{4}{9} + \dfrac{5}{9} =$

(2) $\dfrac{3}{8} + \dfrac{6}{8} =$

(4) $\dfrac{2}{7} + \dfrac{5}{7} =$

3 Chris walks his dog $\dfrac{1}{6}$ of a mile in the morning and $\dfrac{5}{6}$ of a mile in the afternoon. How far did Chris walk his dog altogether?

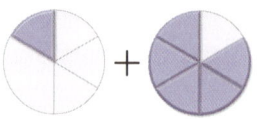

Ans. _____ mile

Check your answers. If you missed any problems, pick one to retry.

8

Name

Date / /

Score / 7

I Add.

(1) $\dfrac{3}{4} + \dfrac{2}{4} =$

(4) $\dfrac{7}{8} + \dfrac{4}{8} =$

(2) $\dfrac{3}{7} + \dfrac{4}{7} =$

(5) $\dfrac{2}{5} + \dfrac{3}{5} =$

(3) $\dfrac{4}{9} + \dfrac{7}{9} =$

(6) $\dfrac{5}{7} + \dfrac{5}{7} =$

2 James walked $\dfrac{2}{8}$ of the way around a track. He stopped for a water break and then walked $\dfrac{7}{8}$ of the way around the track. How many laps of the track did he walk in total?

Ans.   laps

Check your answers.
If you missed any
problems, pick one
to retry.

9

9 Addition
Improper Fractions ①

1 Add.

$$\frac{9}{4} + \frac{2}{4} = \frac{11}{4}$$

$$= 2\frac{3}{4}$$

> Add improper fractions the same way you add proper fractions: add the numerators and keep the denominators as they are.
>
> $$\frac{11}{4} = \frac{8}{4} + \frac{3}{4} = 2 + \frac{3}{4}$$

2 Add.

(1) $\frac{6}{3} + \frac{2}{3} = \frac{8}{3}$

$$= \boxed{}\frac{\boxed{}}{\boxed{}}$$

(2) $\frac{3}{5} + \frac{9}{5} = \frac{\boxed{}}{\boxed{}}$

$$=$$

(3) $\frac{7}{6} + \frac{4}{6} =$

(4) $\frac{6}{4} + \frac{3}{4} =$

3 Tyrone collected $\frac{3}{5}$ of a bucket of seashells on his first day at the beach. He collected $\frac{9}{5}$ buckets of seashells on the second day. How many buckets of seashells did he collect in all?

Ans. _____ buckets of seashells

Name

Date

/ /

Score

/ 7

1 Add.

(1) $\dfrac{5}{3} + \dfrac{8}{3} = \dfrac{\Box}{\Box}$

$= $

(2) $\dfrac{5}{4} + \dfrac{8}{4} = \dfrac{\Box}{\Box}$

$= $

2 Add.

(1) $\dfrac{6}{5} + \dfrac{7}{5} = $

(3) $\dfrac{7}{4} + \dfrac{6}{4} = $

(2) $\dfrac{7}{6} + \dfrac{6}{6} = $

(4) $\dfrac{6}{3} + \dfrac{4}{3} = $

3 A baker uses $\dfrac{3}{2}$ cups of milk and a $\dfrac{1}{2}$ cup of oil. How much liquid does he use in the recipe?

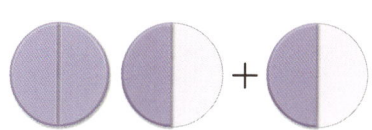

Ans. _____ cups

**Check your answers.
If you missed any
problems, pick one
to retry.**

Name

Date / /

Score / 7

1 Add.

(1) $\dfrac{3}{5} + \dfrac{5}{5} =$

(2) $\dfrac{10}{9} + \dfrac{3}{9} =$

(3) $\dfrac{6}{4} + \dfrac{7}{4} =$

(4) $\dfrac{7}{8} + \dfrac{9}{8} =$

(5) $\dfrac{8}{7} + \dfrac{8}{7} =$

(6) $\dfrac{9}{5} + \dfrac{7}{5} =$

2 Sarah is making cookies. She needs $\dfrac{9}{4}$ teaspoons of baking powder and $\dfrac{6}{4}$ teaspoons of baking soda. How much baking powder and baking soda does she use in the recipe?

Ans.　　　　　　teaspoons

Check your answers.
If you missed any
problems, pick one
to retry.

Name _____ Date ___ / ___ / ___

Score ___ / 9

1 Add.

(1)

$1\dfrac{5}{6} + 2 = 3\dfrac{5}{6}$

(2)

$3 + \dfrac{5}{8} = \boxed{}\dfrac{\boxed{}}{\boxed{}}$

(3)

$2\dfrac{2}{3} + 1 = \boxed{}\dfrac{\boxed{}}{\boxed{}}$

(4)

$2 + \dfrac{3}{10} = \boxed{}\dfrac{\boxed{}}{\boxed{}}$

2 Add.

(1)

$1\dfrac{2}{5} + 3 =$

(2)

$2 + \dfrac{1}{6} =$

(3)

$2\dfrac{3}{4} + 1 =$

(4)

$2 + 2\dfrac{1}{9} =$

3 Jude bought $2\dfrac{3}{4}$ cups of dried black beans and 1 cup of dried kidney beans. How many cups of beans does he have in all?

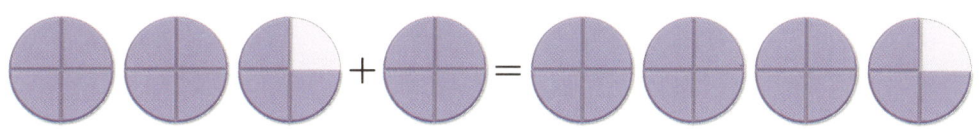

Ans. _____ cups

Name _____ Date __ / __ / __

Score ___ / 7

1 Add.

(1)
$$2\frac{3}{4} + 1 = \boxed{}\frac{\boxed{}}{\boxed{}}$$

(2)
$$1 + 3\frac{3}{5} = \boxed{}\frac{\boxed{}}{\boxed{}}$$

2 Add.

(1)
$$3\frac{3}{7} + 2 =$$

(3)
$$1\frac{1}{6} + 3 =$$

(2)
$$2 + 2\frac{4}{9} =$$

(4)
$$1 + 1\frac{7}{10} =$$

3 Daniel hiked 3 miles in the morning and $\frac{3}{10}$ of a mile in the afternoon. How far did he hike altogether?

Ans. _____ miles

 **Check your answers.**
If you missed any
problems, pick one
to retry.

Name

Date　　/　　/

Score　　/ 9

1 Add.

(1)　$2\dfrac{1}{2} + 2 =$

(2)　$2 + 2\dfrac{4}{5} =$

(3)　$2\dfrac{5}{6} + 1 =$

(4)　$2 + 1\dfrac{9}{10} =$

(5)　$1\dfrac{5}{9} + 2 =$

(6)　$1 + 2\dfrac{7}{8} =$

(7)　$3\dfrac{3}{4} + 1 =$

(8)　$2 + 2\dfrac{2}{7} =$

2 Lola had 2 bags of cat food. Her mom brought home $2\dfrac{4}{7}$ more bags of cat food. How much cat food does Lola have in total?

Ans.　　　　　　bags of food

Check your answers. If you missed any problems, pick one to retry.

15

Name _____ Date ___ / ___ / ___

Score ___ / 9

1 Add.

(1) $1\dfrac{3}{5} + \dfrac{1}{5} = 1\dfrac{4}{5}$

(2) $\dfrac{3}{7} + 2\dfrac{1}{7} = \square\dfrac{\square}{\square}$

(3) $2\dfrac{1}{10} + \dfrac{6}{10} = \square\dfrac{\square}{\square}$

(4) $\dfrac{2}{6} + 1\dfrac{3}{6} = \square\dfrac{\square}{\square}$

2 Add.

(1) $2\dfrac{4}{7} + \dfrac{2}{7} =$

(2) $\dfrac{1}{3} + 3\dfrac{1}{3} =$

(3) $1\dfrac{2}{8} + \dfrac{3}{8} =$

(4) $\dfrac{2}{4} + 2\dfrac{1}{4} =$

3 Aidan has $2\dfrac{4}{7}$ boxes of oranges. His brother gives him $\dfrac{2}{7}$ of a box more. How many boxes of oranges does he have?

Ans. _____ boxes

Addition
Mixed Numbers
Part Two ②

Name _____

Date ___ / ___ / ___

Score ___ / 7

1 Add.

(1)
$$3\frac{2}{4} + \frac{1}{4} = \square\frac{\square}{\square}$$

(2)
$$\frac{4}{7} + 2\frac{1}{7} = \square\frac{\square}{\square}$$

2 Add.

(1)
$$2\frac{3}{5} + \frac{1}{5} =$$

(3)
$$1\frac{3}{10} + \frac{6}{10} =$$

(2)
$$\frac{3}{8} + 2\frac{4}{8} =$$

(4)
$$\frac{2}{9} + 3\frac{3}{9} =$$

3 Jack used $1\frac{2}{8}$ balls of yarn to knit a blanket. Then, he used $\frac{5}{8}$ of a ball of yarn to add a border to the blanket. How many balls of yarn did he use altogether?

Ans. _____ balls of yarn

Check your answers.
If you missed any
problems, pick one
to retry.

17 Addition
Mixed Numbers
Part Three ①

Name

Date   /   /

Score

/ 6

1 Add.

$$1\frac{3}{5} + \frac{4}{5} = 1\frac{7}{5}$$

> When the sum of the fractions is an improper fraction, convert to a mixed number. Then add the whole numbers.

$$1\frac{7}{5} = 1 + \frac{5}{5} + \frac{2}{5}$$
$$= 1 + 1 + \frac{2}{5}$$
$$= 2 + \frac{2}{5}$$

$$= 2\frac{\Box}{\Box}$$

2 Add.

(1) $$1\frac{2}{3} + \frac{2}{3} = \Box\frac{\Box}{\Box}$$

$$=$$

(2) $$2\frac{2}{6} + \frac{5}{6} =$$

(3) $$\frac{5}{9} + 1\frac{6}{9} =$$

(4) $$\frac{4}{5} + 2\frac{2}{5} =$$

3 Corrine spent $\frac{2}{6}$ of an hour preparing cookie batter. It took $2\frac{5}{6}$ hours to bake all the trays of cookies. How much time did it take her to make cookies in all?

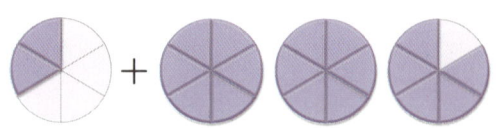

Ans. _____ hours

Name

Date / /

Score / 7

1 Add.

(1) $2\frac{2}{4} + \frac{3}{4} = \square\frac{\square}{\square}$

$= \square\frac{\square}{\square}$

(2) $3\frac{3}{7} + \frac{6}{7} = \square\frac{\square}{\square}$

$= \square\frac{\square}{\square}$

2 Add.

(1) $2\frac{3}{5} + \frac{3}{5} =$

(3) $\frac{5}{7} + 2\frac{3}{7} =$

(2) $1\frac{4}{9} + \frac{7}{9} =$

(4) $\frac{5}{8} + 3\frac{6}{8} =$

3 Tony biked $\frac{3}{5}$ of a mile one day and $1\frac{4}{5}$ miles the next day. How many miles did Tony bike in all?

Ans. _____ miles

Check your answers.
If you missed any
problems, pick one
to retry.

19

Name

Date

/ /

Score

/ 9

1 Add.

(1)

$2\dfrac{1}{3} + 1\dfrac{1}{3} = 3\dfrac{2}{3}$

(3)

$2\dfrac{2}{7} + 2\dfrac{4}{7} = \boxed{}\,\boxed{\dfrac{\boxed{}}{\boxed{}}}$

(2)

$1\dfrac{2}{5} + 3\dfrac{1}{5} = \boxed{}\,\boxed{\dfrac{\boxed{}}{\boxed{}}}$

(4)

$1\dfrac{1}{4} + 3\dfrac{2}{4} = \boxed{}\,\boxed{\dfrac{\boxed{}}{\boxed{}}}$

2 Add.

(1) $2\dfrac{1}{6} + 1\dfrac{4}{6} =$

(3) $2\dfrac{2}{8} + 1\dfrac{3}{8} =$

(2) $1\dfrac{1}{4} + 2\dfrac{2}{4} =$

(4) $2\dfrac{1}{5} + 1\dfrac{3}{5} =$

3 A baker had $1\dfrac{1}{4}$ bags of flour. His assistant bought $2\dfrac{2}{4}$ bags of flour. How much flour does he now have altogether?

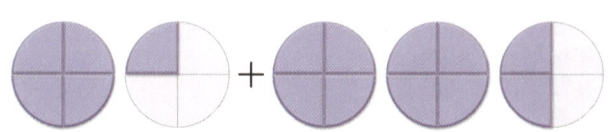

Ans. _____ bags

Name

Date / /

Score / 7

1 Add.

(1) $2\frac{2}{6} + 2\frac{3}{6} = \square\frac{\square}{\square}$

(2) $4\frac{1}{8} + 1\frac{2}{8} = \square\frac{\square}{\square}$

2 Add.

(1) $1\frac{1}{4} + 4\frac{2}{4} =$

(3) $3\frac{2}{5} + 1\frac{1}{5} =$

(2) $2\frac{2}{9} + 2\frac{2}{9} =$

(4) $2\frac{3}{10} + 3\frac{4}{10} =$

3 Lillian read $2\frac{2}{9}$ books in the first week of a summer reading challenge. The second week she read $3\frac{5}{9}$ books. How many books did she read altogether?

Ans. _____ books

**Check your answers.
If you missed any
problems, pick one
to retry.**

Name

Date   /   /

Score

/ 6

1 Add.

$$1\frac{2}{3} + 2\frac{2}{3} = 3\frac{4}{3}$$

$$= 4\frac{\square}{\square}$$

When the sum of the fractions is an improper fraction, convert to a mixed number. Then add the whole numbers.

$$3\frac{4}{3} = 3 + \frac{3}{3} + \frac{1}{3}$$
$$= 3 + 1 + \frac{1}{3}$$
$$= 4 + \frac{1}{3}$$

2 Add.

(1) $2\frac{4}{5} + 1\frac{3}{5} = \square\frac{\square}{\square}$

$$=$$

(3) $2\frac{4}{7} + 1\frac{5}{7} =$

(2) $1\frac{2}{4} + 2\frac{5}{4} =$

(4) $1\frac{3}{6} + 1\frac{4}{6} =$

3 Dante rode his bike $2\frac{4}{5}$ miles to the park. He then rode $1\frac{3}{5}$ more miles to the ice cream shop. How far did he ride in total?

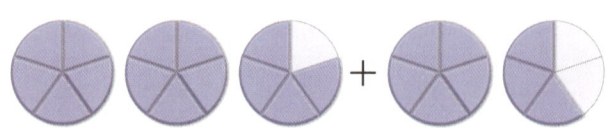

Ans. _____ miles

22 Addition
Mixed Numbers
Part Five ②

Name

Date

/   /

Score

/ 7

1 Add.

(1) $2\dfrac{3}{4} + 1\dfrac{2}{4} = \boxed{}\dfrac{\boxed{}}{\boxed{}}$

$= \boxed{}\dfrac{\boxed{}}{\boxed{}}$

(2) $1\dfrac{3}{5} + 3\dfrac{4}{5} = \boxed{}\dfrac{\boxed{}}{\boxed{}}$

$= \boxed{}\dfrac{\boxed{}}{\boxed{}}$

2 Add.

(1) $1\dfrac{4}{7} + 2\dfrac{4}{7} =$

(3) $2\dfrac{4}{5} + 2\dfrac{4}{5} =$

(2) $2\dfrac{5}{9} + 1\dfrac{6}{9} =$

(4) $1\dfrac{7}{8} + 1\dfrac{2}{8} =$

3 Jared recorded the amount of rain in his town for two days. On the first day, it rained $1\dfrac{3}{6}$ inches and on the second day, it rained $3\dfrac{4}{6}$ inches. How much did it rain in Jared's town over two days?

Ans.   inches

Check your answers.
If you missed any
problems, pick one
to retry.

Name

Date

/   /

Score

/ 6

1 Add.

$$3\frac{2}{3} + 1\frac{1}{3} = 4\frac{3}{3}$$

When the sum of the fractions is an improper fraction with the same numerator and denominator, convert it to a whole number and add it to the other whole number.

$$4\frac{3}{3} = 4 + 1$$

$$= \boxed{}$$

2 Add.

(1) $1\frac{5}{6} + \frac{1}{6} = \boxed{}\,\dfrac{\boxed{}}{\boxed{}}$

$$=$$

(3) $\dfrac{2}{5} + 2\dfrac{3}{5} =$

(2) $2\dfrac{5}{7} + 2\dfrac{2}{7} =$

(4) $2\dfrac{3}{4} + 1\dfrac{1}{4} =$

3 Christine collected $2\frac{5}{7}$ kilograms of tomatoes from her garden in one week. The second week she collected $2\frac{2}{7}$ kilograms of tomatoes. How many kilograms of tomatoes does she have in total?

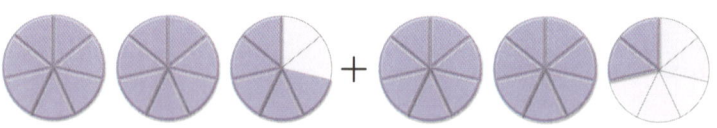

Ans. _____ kilograms

24 **Addition**
The Answer Becomes a
Whole Number ②

Name

Date
/ /

Score
/ 7

1 Add.

(1) $\dfrac{2}{5} + 2\dfrac{3}{5} = \boxed{}\begin{array}{c}\boxed{}\\\boxed{}\end{array}$

$= \boxed{}$

(2) $1\dfrac{4}{6} + 3\dfrac{2}{6} = \boxed{}\begin{array}{c}\boxed{}\\\boxed{}\end{array}$

$= \boxed{}$

2 Add.

(1) $2\dfrac{2}{4} + \dfrac{2}{4} =$

(3) $1\dfrac{6}{8} + 3\dfrac{2}{8} =$

(2) $2\dfrac{8}{9} + 1\dfrac{1}{9} =$

(4) $1\dfrac{2}{7} + 2\dfrac{5}{7} =$

3 Carina has $3\dfrac{5}{8}$ packs of colored paper for an art project. She also has $1\dfrac{3}{8}$ packs of white paper. How much paper does she have altogether for her art project?

Ans. _____ packs of paper

Check your answers.
If you missed any
problems, pick one
to retry.

Name

Date

/ . /

Score

/ 7

1 Add.

(1) $\dfrac{4}{7} + \dfrac{1}{7} =$

(4) $2\dfrac{2}{8} + 1\dfrac{3}{8} =$

(2) $\dfrac{3}{5} + \dfrac{4}{5} =$

(5) $2\dfrac{4}{6} + 2\dfrac{3}{6} =$

(3) $\dfrac{7}{4} + \dfrac{4}{4} =$

(6) $2\dfrac{5}{9} + 1\dfrac{4}{9} =$

2 Ben recorded the growth of his plant over two days. On the first day, the plant grew $1\dfrac{3}{5}$ cm and on the second day, the plant grew $1\dfrac{4}{5}$ cm. How many centimeters did the plant grow in total?

Ans. _____ cm

Check your answers.
If you missed any
problems, pick one
to retry.

Subtraction
Proper Fractions ①

Name

Date /   /

Score

/ 10

1 Subtract.

(1) $\dfrac{3}{5} - \dfrac{1}{5} = \dfrac{2}{5}$

> Just subtract the numerators.
> Leave the denominators as they are.

(2) $\dfrac{2}{4} - \dfrac{1}{4} = \dfrac{\square}{4}$

(3) $\dfrac{2}{3} - \dfrac{1}{3} = \dfrac{\square}{\square}$

(4) $\dfrac{5}{6} - \dfrac{4}{6} = \dfrac{\square}{\square}$

(5) $\dfrac{6}{7} - \dfrac{3}{7} = \dfrac{\square}{\square}$

2 Subtract.

(1) $\dfrac{4}{5} - \dfrac{2}{5} =$

(2) $\dfrac{3}{6} - \dfrac{2}{6} =$

(3) $\dfrac{3}{4} - \dfrac{2}{4} =$

(4) $\dfrac{4}{5} - \dfrac{1}{5} =$

3 A chef has $\dfrac{2}{3}$ of a cup of milk for his recipe. He uses $\dfrac{1}{3}$ of a cup for a sauce. How much milk is leftover?

$\dfrac{2}{3} - \dfrac{1}{3} = \dfrac{\square}{\square}$

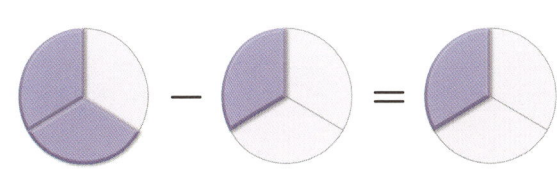

Ans. _____ of a cup

Name

Date   /   /

Score   / 9

1 Subtract.

(1) $\dfrac{4}{6} - \dfrac{3}{6} = \dfrac{\square}{\square}$

(3) $\dfrac{5}{8} - \dfrac{2}{8} = \dfrac{\square}{\square}$

(2) $\dfrac{4}{7} - \dfrac{1}{7} = \dfrac{\square}{\square}$

(4) $\dfrac{4}{9} - \dfrac{2}{9} = \dfrac{\square}{\square}$

2 Subtract.

(1) $\dfrac{6}{7} - \dfrac{4}{7} =$

(3) $\dfrac{3}{10} - \dfrac{2}{10} =$

(2) $\dfrac{5}{9} - \dfrac{3}{9} =$

(4) $\dfrac{5}{7} - \dfrac{2}{7} =$

3 Maddox has $\dfrac{7}{10}$ of a yard of fabric. He uses $\dfrac{4}{10}$ of a yard to make a pillowcase. How many yards does he have left?

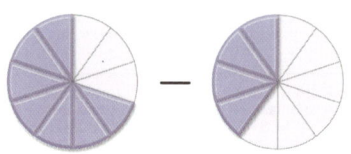

Ans. _____ of a yard

Check your answers. If you missed any problems, pick one to retry.

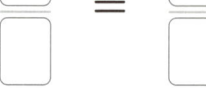

Name

Date

Score

/ 9

1 Subtract.

(1) $\dfrac{3}{4} - \dfrac{2}{4} =$

(5) $\dfrac{4}{5} - \dfrac{3}{5} =$

(2) $\dfrac{5}{6} - \dfrac{4}{6} =$

(6) $\dfrac{7}{10} - \dfrac{4}{10} =$

(3) $\dfrac{8}{9} - \dfrac{7}{9} =$

(7) $\dfrac{5}{8} - \dfrac{4}{8} =$

(4) $\dfrac{5}{7} - \dfrac{3}{7} =$

(8) $\dfrac{8}{9} - \dfrac{6}{9} =$

2 Madeline has $\dfrac{6}{8}$ of a yard of ribbon. She uses $\dfrac{3}{8}$ of a yard to make a hair bow for her sister. How much ribbon does she have left?

Ans. _____ of a yard

Check your answers. If you missed any problems, pick one to retry.

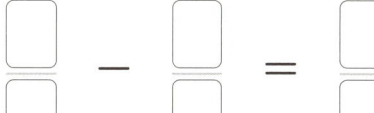

Name

Date   /   /

Score

/ 6

1 Subtract.

$$\frac{8}{3} - \frac{4}{3} = \frac{4}{3}$$

$$= 1\frac{1}{3}$$

> Subtract improper fractions the same way you subtract proper fractions. When the answer is a improper fraction, convert it to a mixed number or a whole number.
>
> $$\frac{4}{3} = \frac{3}{3} + \frac{1}{3} = 1 + \frac{1}{3}$$

2 Subtract.

(1) $\dfrac{5}{3} - \dfrac{4}{3} = \dfrac{\square}{\square}$

(3) $\dfrac{10}{7} - \dfrac{6}{7} =$

(2) $\dfrac{12}{5} - \dfrac{6}{5} = \dfrac{6}{5}$

$$= \square\dfrac{\square}{\square}$$

(4) $\dfrac{9}{6} - \dfrac{2}{6} =$

3 Peyton has $\frac{12}{5}$ ml of dye. She uses $\frac{6}{5}$ ml to dye a shirt. How much dye does she have left?

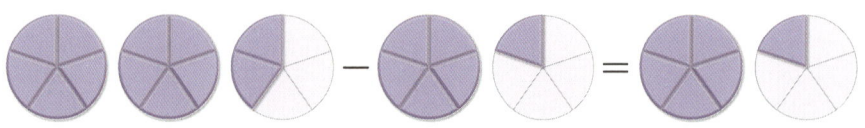

Ans.   ml

Subtraction
Improper Fractions ②

Name

Date

/ /

Score

/ 7

1 Subtract.

(1) $\dfrac{12}{4} - \dfrac{5}{4} = \dfrac{\boxed{}}{\boxed{}}$

$= $

(2) $\dfrac{8}{3} - \dfrac{2}{3} = \dfrac{\boxed{}}{\boxed{}}$

$= 2$

2 Subtract.

(1) $\dfrac{14}{5} - \dfrac{7}{5} = $

(3) $\dfrac{13}{4} - \dfrac{5}{4} = $

(2) $\dfrac{12}{2} - \dfrac{10}{2} = $

(4) $\dfrac{13}{4} - \dfrac{4}{4} = $

3 A baker has $\dfrac{8}{3}$ loaves of bread. $\dfrac{1}{3}$ of a loaf is stale. How many loaves does she have left?

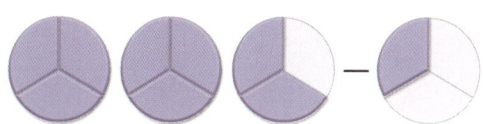

Ans.   loaves

Check your answers.
If you missed any
problems, pick one
to retry.

Subtraction
Improper Fractions ③

Name

Date   /   /

Score   / 7

1 Subtract.

(1) $\dfrac{14}{5} - \dfrac{6}{5} =$

(4) $\dfrac{15}{6} - \dfrac{8}{6} =$

(2) $\dfrac{13}{3} - \dfrac{7}{3} =$

(5) $\dfrac{15}{9} - \dfrac{6}{9} =$

(3) $\dfrac{13}{2} - \dfrac{8}{2} =$

(6) $\dfrac{14}{3} - \dfrac{6}{3} =$

2 Daniel had $\dfrac{13}{6}$ pounds of clay. He used $\dfrac{7}{6}$ pounds to make a vase. How many pounds of clay does he have left?

Ans. _____ pound

Check your answers.
If you missed any
problems, pick one
to retry.

Name

Date
/ /

Score
/ 10

1 Subtract.

(1) $3\dfrac{1}{4} - 2 = 1\dfrac{1}{4}$

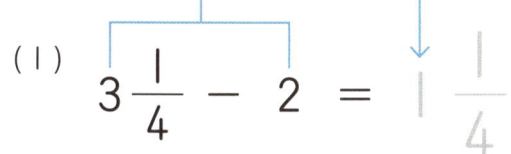

Subtract the whole numbers.
Then subtract the fractions.

(2) $4\dfrac{2}{3} - 3 = \dfrac{\square}{\square}$

(4) $2\dfrac{3}{5} - 2 = \dfrac{3}{5}$

(3) $2\dfrac{3}{4} - 1 = \dfrac{\square}{\square}$

(5) $4\dfrac{5}{6} - 4 = \dfrac{\square}{\square}$

2 Subtract.

(1) $2\dfrac{3}{8} - 1 =$

(3) $3\dfrac{1}{6} - 3 =$

(2) $3\dfrac{2}{7} - 1 =$

(4) $2\dfrac{4}{9} - 2 =$

3 TJ has $3\dfrac{1}{4}$ pints of ice cream. He shared 2 pints with his friends. How much ice cream does he have left?

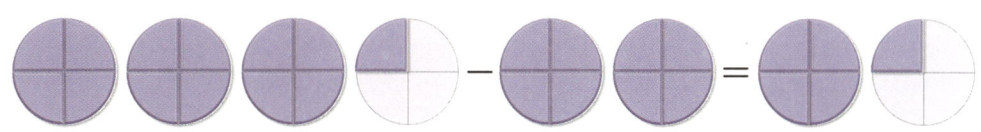

Ans.   pints

Name

Date / /

Score / 9

1 Subtract.

(1) $2\dfrac{1}{2} - 1 =$

(2) $3\dfrac{2}{3} - 3 =$

(3) $1\dfrac{1}{6} - 1 =$

(4) $3\dfrac{2}{5} - 1 =$

(5) $4\dfrac{6}{7} - 2 =$

(6) $2\dfrac{3}{4} - 2 =$

(7) $2\dfrac{3}{8} - 2 =$

(8) $5\dfrac{7}{9} - 4 =$

2 Ruby poured $2\dfrac{4}{5}$ cups of oil into a measuring cup. Then, she poured 2 cups into a mixing bowl. How much oil is left in the measuring cup?

Ans. _____ of a cup

Check your answers.
If you missed any
problems, pick one
to retry.

Name

Date   /   /

Score   / 8

1 Subtract.

(1)

$1\dfrac{4}{5} - \dfrac{2}{5} = 1\dfrac{2}{5}$

Write the whole number.
Then subtract the fractions.

(2) $2\dfrac{3}{4} - \dfrac{2}{4} = \boxed{}\dfrac{\boxed{}}{\boxed{}}$

(3) $4\dfrac{2}{3} - \dfrac{2}{3} = 4$

2 Subtract.

(1) $3\dfrac{5}{6} - \dfrac{4}{6} =$

(3) $3\dfrac{3}{4} - \dfrac{3}{4} =$

(2) $2\dfrac{4}{9} - \dfrac{3}{9} =$

(4) $2\dfrac{6}{7} - \dfrac{6}{7} =$

3 Joanna has $2\dfrac{4}{9}$ hours to complete a project. She spends $\dfrac{3}{9}$ of an hour preparing her materials. How much time does she have left to complete the project?

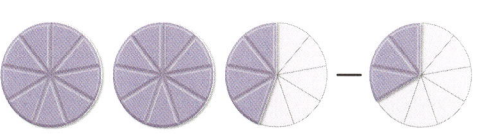

Ans. _____ hours

35 Subtraction
Mixed Numbers
Part Two ②

1 Subtract.

(1) $1\frac{5}{7} - \frac{2}{7} = \boxed{}\begin{array}{c}\boxed{}\\\boxed{}\end{array}$

(2) $3\frac{4}{8} - \frac{4}{8} = \boxed{}$

2 Subtract.

(1) $1\frac{2}{9} - \frac{2}{9} =$

(3) $1\frac{7}{10} - \frac{4}{10} =$

(2) $4\frac{4}{6} - \frac{3}{6} =$

(4) $3\frac{2}{5} - \frac{2}{5} =$

3 Sal has $2\frac{6}{8}$ pounds of carrots. He sells $\frac{3}{8}$ of a pound at his farm stand. How many pounds of carrots does he have left?

Ans. _____ pounds

Check your answers. If you missed any problems, pick one to retry.

36 Subtraction
Mixed Numbers
Part Three ①

Name

Date   /   /

Score

/ 6

1 Subtract.

$$1\frac{1}{4} - \frac{2}{4} = \frac{5}{4} - \frac{2}{4}$$

$$= \frac{3}{4}$$

> Convert $1\frac{1}{4}$ to $\frac{5}{4}$.
>
> $$1\frac{1}{4} = 1 + \frac{1}{4}$$
> $$= \frac{4}{4} + \frac{1}{4}$$
>
> Then calculate.

2 Subtract.

(1) $$1\frac{2}{5} - \frac{3}{5} = \frac{7}{5} - \frac{3}{5}$$

$$=$$

(2) $$1\frac{4}{6} - \frac{5}{6} = \frac{\square}{\square} - \frac{5}{6}$$

$$=$$

(3) $$1\frac{3}{9} - \frac{8}{9} =$$

(4) $$1\frac{3}{8} - \frac{6}{8} =$$

3 Leah has $1\frac{4}{6}$ feet of ribbon. She used $\frac{5}{6}$ of a foot to trim a blouse. How much ribbon does she have left?

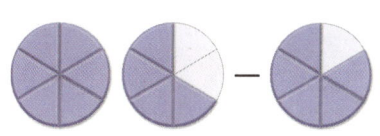

Ans. _____ of a foot

37

Subtraction
Mixed Numbers
Part Three ②

Name

Date
/ /

Score
/ 7

1 Subtract.

(1) $2\dfrac{1}{3} - \dfrac{2}{3} = 1\dfrac{4}{3} - \dfrac{2}{3}$

$= \boxed{}\dfrac{\boxed{}}{\boxed{}}$

(2) $3\dfrac{3}{5} - \dfrac{4}{5} = 2\dfrac{8}{5} - \dfrac{4}{5}$

$= \boxed{}\dfrac{\boxed{}}{\boxed{}}$

2 Subtract.

(1) $3\dfrac{2}{6} - \dfrac{3}{6} = \boxed{}\dfrac{\boxed{}}{\boxed{}} - \dfrac{3}{6}$

$=$

(3) $2\dfrac{2}{10} - \dfrac{5}{10} =$

(2) $4\dfrac{4}{7} - \dfrac{5}{7} =$

(4) $3\dfrac{2}{4} - \dfrac{3}{4} =$

3 John has $4\dfrac{1}{5}$ grams of candy. He gives his friend $\dfrac{4}{5}$ of a gram of candy. How many grams of candy does John have left?

Ans.   grams of candy

Check your answers.
If you missed any
problems, pick one
to retry.

Name

Date   /   /

Score   / 8

1 Subtract.

(1)

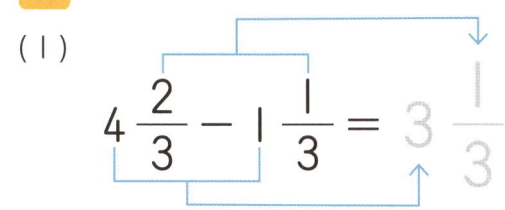

$4\dfrac{2}{3} - 1\dfrac{1}{3} = 3\dfrac{1}{3}$

> Subtract the whole numbers.
> Then subtract the fractions.

(2) $2\dfrac{3}{5} - 2\dfrac{1}{5} = \dfrac{\Box}{\Box}$

(3) $4\dfrac{5}{6} - 2\dfrac{5}{6} = \Box$

2 Subtract.

(1) $3\dfrac{4}{6} - 1\dfrac{3}{6} =$

(3) $3\dfrac{3}{6} - 3\dfrac{2}{6} =$

(2) $2\dfrac{6}{7} - 1\dfrac{2}{7} =$

(4) $3\dfrac{1}{2} - 2\dfrac{1}{2} =$

3 Vincent spent $3\dfrac{4}{6}$ hours studying science and $1\dfrac{3}{6}$ hours studying math. How much more time did he spend studying science than math?

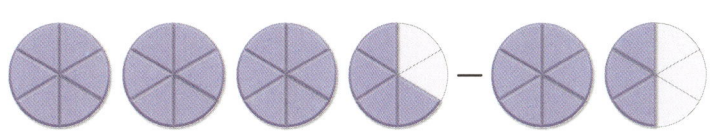

Ans. _____ hours

39

Name

Date
/   /

Score
/ 7

1 Subtract.

(1)
$$3\frac{7}{8} - 2\frac{2}{8} = \boxed{}\frac{\boxed{}}{\boxed{}}$$

(2)
$$3\frac{7}{9} - 3\frac{5}{9} = \frac{\boxed{}}{\boxed{}}$$

2 Subtract.

(1)
$$4\frac{5}{7} - 2\frac{5}{7} =$$

(3)
$$3\frac{4}{5} - 1\frac{3}{5} =$$

(2)
$$1\frac{3}{6} - 1\frac{2}{6} =$$

(4)
$$4\frac{2}{4} - 1\frac{1}{4} =$$

3 Zara has $4\frac{5}{9}$ meters of tape. She cut $2\frac{3}{9}$ meters for a project. How much tape does she have left?

Ans. _____ meters of tape

Check your answers.
If you missed any
problems, pick one
to retry.

Subtraction
Mixed Numbers
Part Five ①

1 Subtract.

$$3\frac{2}{5} - 1\frac{4}{5} = 2\frac{7}{5} - 1\frac{4}{5}$$

$$= 1\frac{\boxed{}}{\boxed{}}$$

> When you cannot subtract the fractions as they are, convert the mixed number to an improper fraction.
> $$3\frac{2}{5} = 2\frac{2}{5} + 1$$
> $$= 2\frac{2}{5} + \frac{5}{5} = 2 + \frac{7}{5}$$
> Then calculate.

2 Subtract.

(1) $$4\frac{1}{3} - 1\frac{2}{3} = 3\frac{\boxed{}}{\boxed{}} - 1\frac{2}{3}$$

$$=$$

(2) $$2\frac{2}{4} - 1\frac{3}{4} = 1\frac{\boxed{}}{\boxed{}} - 1\frac{3}{4}$$

$$=$$

(3) $$3\frac{1}{7} - 1\frac{5}{7} =$$

(4) $$3\frac{4}{6} - 2\frac{5}{6} =$$

3 Lincoln collected $4\frac{1}{3}$ quarts of milk. He used $1\frac{2}{3}$ quarts to make cheese. How many quarts of milk does he have left?

Ans. _____ quarts

Name _____ Date __/__/__

Score ___/ 7

1 Subtract.

(1) $5\dfrac{4}{6} - 3\dfrac{5}{6} = 4\dfrac{\Box}{\Box} - 3\dfrac{5}{6}$

$= \Box\dfrac{\Box}{\Box}$

(2) $3\dfrac{2}{9} - 2\dfrac{4}{9} = 2\dfrac{\Box}{\Box} - 2\dfrac{4}{9}$

$= \dfrac{\Box}{\Box}$

2 Subtract.

(1) $4\dfrac{3}{7} - 1\dfrac{6}{7} =$

(3) $2\dfrac{1}{5} - 1\dfrac{3}{5} =$

(2) $4\dfrac{3}{8} - 2\dfrac{4}{8} =$

(4) $3\dfrac{1}{3} - 2\dfrac{2}{3} =$

3 Viviane bought $3\dfrac{2}{4}$ yards of rope for a swing. She used $2\dfrac{3}{4}$ yards to hang the swing from a tree. How much rope does she have left?

Ans. _____ of a yard

Check your answers.
If you missed any
problems, pick one
to retry.

Subtraction
Whole Number —
Proper Fraction ①

Name

Date   /   /

Score   / 6

1 Subtract.

$$2 - \frac{3}{5} = 1\frac{5}{5} - \frac{3}{5}$$

$$= 1\frac{2}{5}$$

> Convert 2 to $1\frac{5}{5}$.
>
> $2 = 1 + 1$
>
> $= 1 + \frac{5}{5}$
>
> Then calculate.

2 Subtract.

(1) $1 - \frac{3}{8} = \frac{8}{8} - \frac{3}{8}$

$=$

(2) $2 - \frac{1}{4} = 1\frac{\square}{\square} - \frac{1}{4}$

$=$

(3) $1 - \frac{4}{5} =$

(4) $2 - \frac{1}{6} =$

3 Lance has 3 crates of peppers. $\frac{1}{4}$ of a crate is spoiled. How many crates of peppers does he have left?

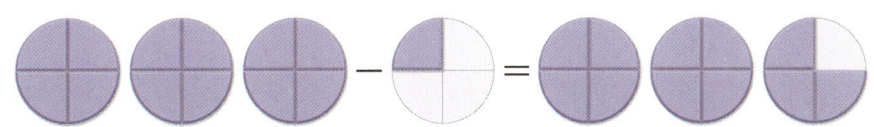

Ans. _____ crates

43

Subtraction
Whole Number —
Proper Fraction ②

1 Subtract.

(1)
$$3 - \frac{1}{3} = 2\frac{3}{3} - \frac{1}{3}$$
$$= \boxed{}\frac{\boxed{}}{\boxed{}}$$

(2)
$$4 - \frac{2}{5} = 3\frac{5}{5} - \frac{2}{5}$$
$$= \boxed{}\frac{\boxed{}}{\boxed{}}$$

2 Subtract.

(1)
$$3 - \frac{3}{7} = \boxed{}\frac{\boxed{}}{\boxed{}} - \frac{3}{7}$$
$$=$$

(3)
$$4 - \frac{7}{10} =$$

(2)
$$3 - \frac{2}{3} =$$

(4)
$$4 - \frac{3}{8} =$$

3 Emily made 3 apple pies. $\frac{7}{10}$ of a pie were eaten. How much of the pies are left?

Ans. _____ pies

**Check your answers.
If you missed any
problems, pick one
to retry.**

44

Subtraction
Whole Number — Proper Fraction ③

Name

Date / /

Score / 7

1 Subtract.

(1) $1 - \dfrac{7}{9} =$

(4) $3 - \dfrac{5}{8} =$

(2) $2 - \dfrac{3}{4} =$

(5) $4 - \dfrac{2}{3} =$

(3) $2 - \dfrac{1}{10} =$

(6) $3 - \dfrac{1}{6} =$

2 Colin has a whole pizza. He eats $\dfrac{3}{8}$. How much of the pizza is left?

Ans. _____ of the pizza

**Check your answers.
If you missed any
problems, pick one
to retry.**

Subtraction
Whole Number — Mixed Number ①

1 Subtract.

$$3 - 1\frac{2}{5} = 2\frac{5}{5} - 1\frac{2}{5}$$

$$= 1\frac{3}{5}$$

> Convert 3 to $2\frac{5}{5}$.
>
> $3 = 2 + 1$
>
> $= 2 + \frac{5}{5}$
>
> Then calculate.

2 Subtract.

(1) $$2 - 1\frac{3}{7} = 1\frac{7}{7} - 1\frac{3}{7}$$

$$=$$

(3) $$3 - 2\frac{5}{6} =$$

(2) $$3 - 1\frac{3}{4} = 2\frac{\square}{\square} - 1\frac{3}{4}$$

$$=$$

(4) $$2 - \frac{4}{9} =$$

3 Yvette has 3 gallons of salt water to fill her small fish tanks. She uses $1\frac{3}{4}$ gallons for the first tank. How much salt water does she have left for the second tank?

Ans. _____ gallons

Subtraction
Whole Number —
Mixed Number ②

Name

Date

/ /

Score

/ 7

1 Subtract.

(1)
$$4 - 1\frac{1}{4} = 3\frac{4}{4} - 1\frac{1}{4}$$

$$= \boxed{}\frac{\boxed{}}{\boxed{}}$$

(2)
$$5 - 2\frac{3}{8} = 4\frac{8}{8} - 2\frac{3}{8}$$

$$= \boxed{}\frac{\boxed{}}{\boxed{}}$$

2 Subtract.

(1)
$$3 - 1\frac{1}{6} = \boxed{}\frac{\boxed{}}{\boxed{}} - 1\frac{1}{6}$$

$$=$$

(3)
$$4 - 1\frac{2}{7} =$$

(2)
$$4 - 2\frac{7}{10} =$$

(4)
$$5 - 1\frac{4}{5} =$$

3 Mei has 3 yards of flannel fabric. She uses $2\frac{5}{9}$ yards to make a blanket. How many yards does she have left?

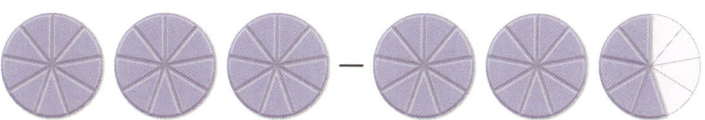

Ans. _____ of a yard

Check your answers.
If you missed any
problems, pick one
to retry.

47 Subtraction
Whole Number —
Mixed Number ③

1 Subtract.

(1) $2 - 1\dfrac{1}{8} =$

(4) $3 - 2\dfrac{1}{7} =$

(2) $5 - 2\dfrac{1}{3} =$

(5) $5 - 1\dfrac{3}{10} =$

(3) $4 - 2\dfrac{5}{9} =$

(6) $4 - 1\dfrac{3}{4} =$

2 Carter has 3 pounds of flour. He uses $1\dfrac{1}{6}$ pounds to make bread. How much flour does he have left?

Ans.   pounds of flour

**Check your answers.
If you missed any
problems, pick one
to retry.**

48

Subtraction
Mixed

Name _____

Date ___ / ___ / ___

Score ___ / 7

1 Subtract.

(1) $\dfrac{4}{6} - \dfrac{3}{6} =$

(4) $2\dfrac{3}{7} - \dfrac{5}{7} =$

(2) $\dfrac{13}{5} - \dfrac{6}{5} =$

(5) $3\dfrac{1}{9} - 1\dfrac{3}{9} =$

(3) $3\dfrac{9}{10} - 3 =$

(6) $4 - 1\dfrac{3}{4} =$

2 Pauline wants to hike a trail that is $1\dfrac{2}{4}$ miles long. She hikes $\dfrac{3}{4}$ of a mile of the way in the morning. How much farther does she have to hike in the afternoon?

Ans. _____ of a mile

Check your answers.
If you missed any
problems, pick one
to retry.

Name

Date   /   /

Score   / 5

1 Write > (greater than), or < (less than) to compare the decimals.

(1)

0 . 1   0 . 5

(2)

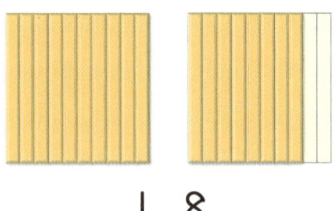      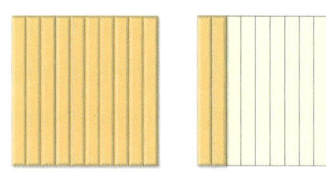

1 . 8   1 . 2

(3)

    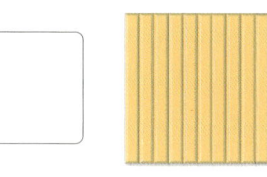   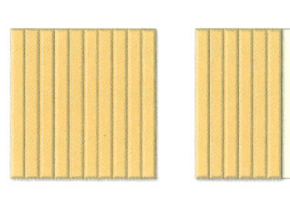

2 . 3   2 . 6

2 Write the values of A, B, and C as shown on the number line .

(1)

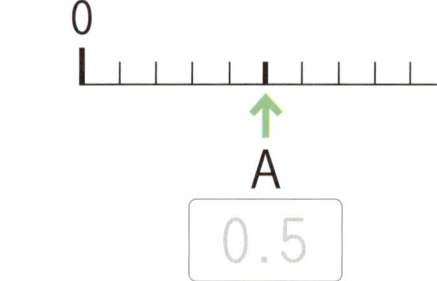

0.5

(2)

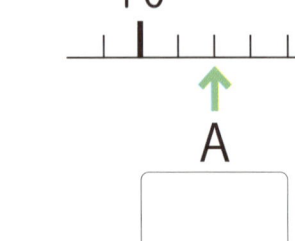

1 Write > (greater than), < (less than), or = (equal to) to compare the decimals.

(1)

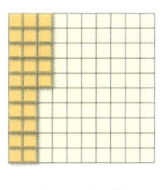

0 . 25

0 . 75

(2)

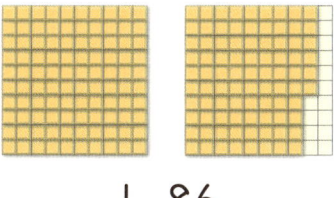

1 . 86

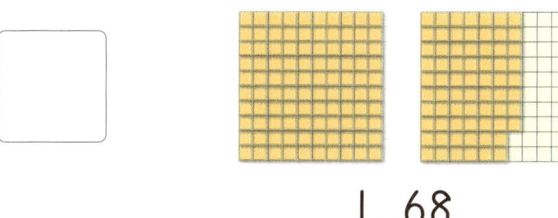

1 . 68

(3)

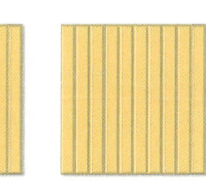

2 . 5

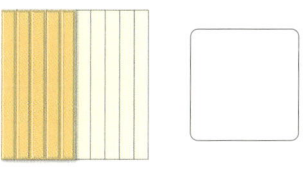

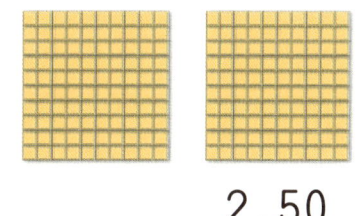

2 . 50

2 Write the values of A, B, and C as shown on the number line .

(1)

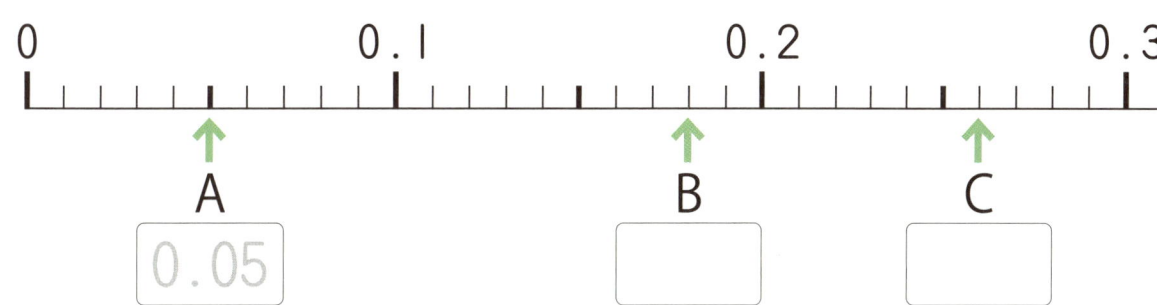

A
0.05

B

C

(2)

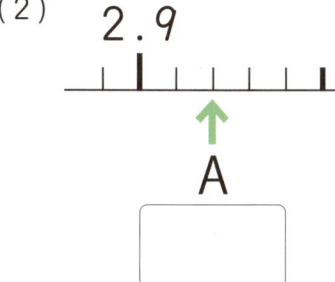

A

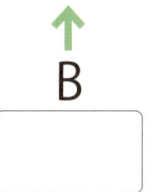

B

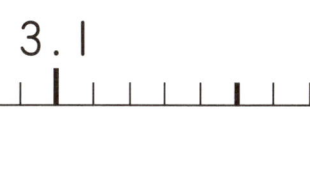

C

51 Addition
Up to Tenths Place ①

1 Add.

(1) 1.2 + 0.6 = 1.8

(2) 1.3 + 1.5 = ☐

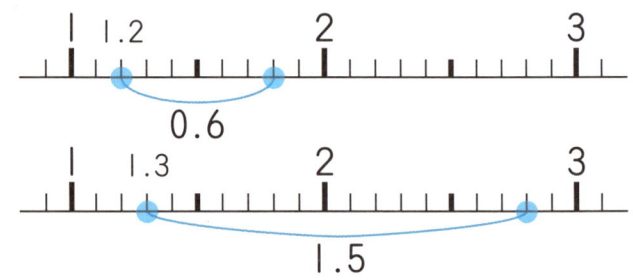

2 Add.

(1)
```
   2.3
 + 0.5
 ------
   2.8
```

(2)
```
   3.3
 + 0.5
 ------
```

(3)
```
   0.5
 + 7.1
 ------
```

(4)
```
   0.6
 + 0.3
 ------
```

(5)
```
   5
 + 4.4
 ------
```

(6)
```
   1.4
 + 1.7
 ------
```

3 Keith uses 3.3 grams of blue food coloring and 0.5 grams of yellow food coloring to make green icing. How many grams of food coloring did he use in all?

3.3 + 0.5 = ☐

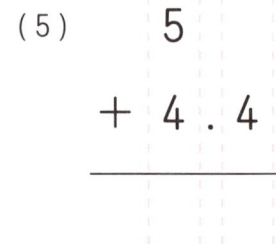

Ans. _____ grams

52 Addition
Up to Tenths Place ②

Name

Date
/ /

Score
/ 9

1 Add.

(1) 1 + 0.9 =

(2) 2.6 + 1.5 =

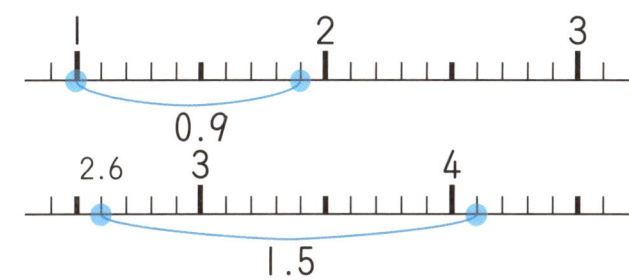

2 Add.

(1)
```
   0 . 9
 + 1 . 3
 ───────
   2 . 2
```

(2)
```
   0 . 8
 + 8 . 1
 ───────
```

(3)
```
   2
 + 0 . 9
 ───────
```

(4)
```
   2 . 1
 + 1 . 8
 ───────
```

(5)
```
   0 . 8
 + 0 . 7
 ───────
```

(6)
```
   4 . 3
 + 0 . 9
 ───────
```

3 Jeanette uses 0.6 feet of yellow ribbon and 1.5 feet of blue ribbon to make a bow for a hat. How much ribbon did she use in total?

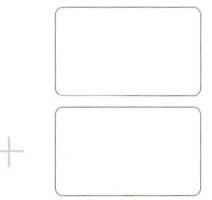

Check your answers.
If you missed any problems, pick one to retry.

☐
+ ☐

Ans. _____ feet of ribbon

Name

Date   /   /

Score   / 11

1 Add.

(1) 3.3 + 0.4 =

(2) 0.9 + 0.4 =

(3) 3 + 2.5 =

(4) 1.2 + 4 =

2 Add.

(1)   0.8
    + 0.5
    _____

(2)   2.5
    + 1.2
    _____

(3)   0.4
    + 2.7
    _____

(4)   3.6
    + 0.6
    _____

(5)   1.9
    + 2.2
    _____

(6)   0.6
    + 1.8
    _____

3 Oliver has 1.5 oz of milk chocolate and 0.8 oz of dark chocolate. How much chocolate does he have altogether?

Ans. _____ oz

Check your answers. If you missed any problems, pick one to retry.

Check & Fix

+

54

Addition
Up to Hundredths Place
Part One ①

Name

Date / /

Score / 9

1 Add.

(1)
```
    0 . 3 7
  + 0 . 4 5
  _____
    0 . 8 2
```

> Calculate like whole numbers. Align the numbers and the decimal points.
> Remember to write 0 in the ones column and include the decimal point in your answer.

(2)
```
    0 . 4 9
  + 0 . 1 2
  _____
```

2 Add.

(1)
```
    0 . 5 1
  + 0 . 0 5
  _____
```

(3)
```
    0 . 3 7
  + 0 . 4 5
  _____
```

(5)
```
    0 . 3 4
  + 0 . 3 9
  _____
```

(2)
```
    0 . 6 2
  + 0 . 3 3
  _____
```

(4)
```
    0 . 7 5
  + 0 . 1 2
  _____
```

(6)
```
    0 . 1 9
  + 0 . 4 2
  _____
```

3 Jeffery biked 0.37 miles to the library and then another 0.45 miles to the post office. How far did he bike in total?

Ans. _____ miles

Name

Date   /   /

Score

/10

1 Add.

(1)
```
    0 . 6 2
+   0 . 4 9
─────────
    1 . 1 1
```

(2)
```
    0 . 5 3
+   0 . 5 2
─────────
```

(3)
```
    0 . 2 7
+   0 . 6 6
─────────
```

2 Add.

(1)
```
    0.64
+   0.91
───────
```

(3)
```
    0.34
+   0.58
───────
```

(5)
```
    0.28
+   0.81
───────
```

(2)
```
    0.16
+   0.87
───────
```

(4)
```
    0.25
+   0.07
───────
```

(6)
```
    0.77
+   0.54
───────
```

3 Sasha measured the growth of his plant.
It grew 0.57 cm on Day 1 and 0.86 cm on
Day 2. How many centimeters did his plant
grow in two days?

Check your answers.
If you missed any problems, pick one to retry.

Check & Fix

Ans. _____ cm

56

Addition
Up to Hundredths Place
Part One ③

Name

Date
/ /

Score
/ 10

1 Add.

(1)
```
  0.64
+ 0.22
```

(4)
```
  0.82
+ 0.72
```

(7)
```
  0.43
+ 0.75
```

(2)
```
  0.96
+ 0.06
```

(5)
```
  0.48
+ 0.35
```

(8)
```
  0.96
+ 0.07
```

(3)
```
  0.18
+ 0.44
```

(6)
```
  0.73
+ 0.52
```

(9)
```
  0.37
+ 0.45
```

2 Eloise bought a cantaloupe that was 0.41 kilograms and a watermelon that was 0.95 kilograms. How much do the two melons weigh altogether?

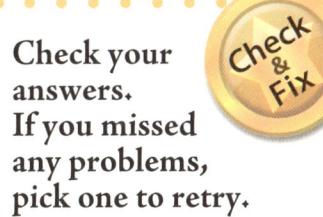

Check your answers. If you missed any problems, pick one to retry.

Ans. _____ kilograms

Name

Date   /   /

Score   / 9

1 Add.

(1)
```
    1 . 2 8
  + 3 . 5 3
  ─────────
    4 . 8 1
```

> Calculate like whole numbers.
> Align the numbers and the decimal points.
> Remember to write the decimal point in your answer.

(2)
```
    2 . 3 1
  + 1 . 2 7
  ─────────
```

2 Add.

(1)
```
    4 . 1 6
  + 3 . 2 2
  ─────────
```

(3)
```
    6 . 5 4
  + 0 . 4 3
  ─────────
```

(5)
```
    1 . 6 4
  + 4 . 5 5
  ─────────
```

(2)
```
    2 . 4 7
  + 6 . 1 2
  ─────────
```

(4)
```
    0 . 9 1
  + 3 . 3 5
  ─────────
```

(6)
```
    3 . 2 8
  + 4 . 2 3
  ─────────
```

3 A farmer planted 2.47 km² of corn and 6.12 km² of carrots. How much of his land did he plant?

Ans. _____ km²

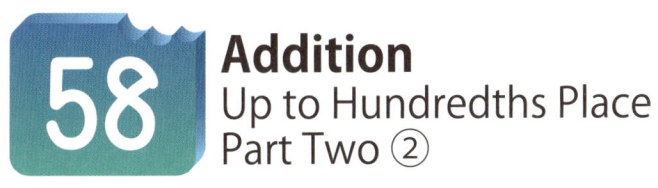

58 Addition
Up to Hundredths Place
Part Two ②

Score / 10

1 Add.

(1)
```
    5 . 1 5
  + 2 . 6 6
  ─────────
    7 . 8 1
```

(2)
```
    1 . 9 6
  + 0 . 5 3
  ─────────
```

(3)
```
    4 . 5 8
  + 4 . 1 5
  ─────────
```

2 Add.

(1)
```
    6 . 2 9
  + 1 . 8 2
  ─────────
```

(3)
```
    4 . 1 3
  + 3 . 4 5
  ─────────
```

(5)
```
    6 . 5 7
  + 0 . 3 4
  ─────────
```

(2)
```
    0 . 0 2
  + 3 . 1 9
  ─────────
```

(4)
```
    2 . 9 7
  + 4 . 2 5
  ─────────
```

(6)
```
    0 . 0 8
  + 8 . 9 8
  ─────────
```

3 Brittany used 1.28 gallons of water to water her plants on Day 1 and 3.53 gallons of water on Day 2. How many gallons of water did she use over the two days?

Check your answers. If you missed any problems, pick one to retry.

Check & Fix

Ans. _____ gallons

59

59 Addition
Up to Hundredths Place
Part Two ③

1 Add.

(1)   1.52
    + 1.74
    ‾‾‾‾‾‾

(4)   6.46
    + 1.55
    ‾‾‾‾‾‾

(7)   7.61
    + 0.58
    ‾‾‾‾‾‾

(2)   3.28
    + 1.81
    ‾‾‾‾‾‾

(5)   7.44
    + 0.82
    ‾‾‾‾‾‾

(8)   5.78
    + 3.26
    ‾‾‾‾‾‾

(3)   4.25
    + 3.52
    ‾‾‾‾‾‾

(6)   5.63
    + 2.08
    ‾‾‾‾‾‾

(9)   1.95
    + 6.29
    ‾‾‾‾‾‾

2 Eli caught one fish that weighed 1.36 pounds and a second fish that weighed 4.15 pounds. How many pounds of fish did he catch?

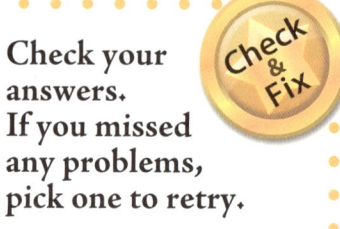

Check your answers. If you missed any problems, pick one to retry.

Ans. _____ pounds

60
Addition
Up to Thousandths Place
Part One ①

Name

Date
　　／　／

Score
　　／9

1 Add.

(1)
```
   0 . 4 6 5
 + 0 . 3 8 7
 ───────────
   0 . 8 5 2
```

Calculate like whole numbers. Align the numbers and the decimal points.
Remember to write 0 in the ones column and include the decimal point in your answer.

(2)
```
   0 . 3 1 2
 + 0 . 3 4 9
 ───────────
```

2 Add.

(1)
```
   0 . 6 4 9
 + 0 . 2 2 4
 ───────────
```

(3)
```
   0 . 1 7 6
 + 0 . 2 5 8
 ───────────
```

(5)
```
   0 . 5 7 1
 + 0 . 2 3 5
 ───────────
```

(2)
```
   0 . 2 3 4
 + 0 . 4 4 5
 ───────────
```

(4)
```
   0 . 6 9 8
 + 0 . 2 2 1
 ───────────
```

(6)
```
   0 . 1 6 3
 + 0 . 6 6 2
 ───────────
```

3 A truck is carrying 0.176 tons of lumber and 0.258 tons of pipe. How much weight is the truck carrying altogether?

Ans. _____ tons

61 Addition
Up to Thousandths Place
Part One ②

Name

Date
/ /

Score
/ 10

1 Add.

(1)
```
   0 . 0 1 5
 + 0 . 7 2 9
 ───────────
   0 . 7 4 4
```

(2)
```
   0 . 2 9 1
 + 0 . 3 2 1
 ───────────
```

(3)
```
   0 . 6 3 4
 + 0 . 0 2 7
 ───────────
```

2 Add.

(1)
```
   0 . 2 4 9
 + 0 . 4 1 5
 ───────────
```

(3)
```
   0 . 0 0 7
 + 0 . 1 8 4
 ───────────
```

(5)
```
   0 . 8 8 1
 + 0 . 0 3 8
 ───────────
```

(2)
```
   0 . 3 0 8
 + 0 . 5 1 7
 ───────────
```

(4)
```
   0 . 3 5 8
 + 0 . 0 4 3
 ───────────
```

(6)
```
   0 . 5 2 4
 + 0 . 2 0 7
 ───────────
```

3 Xavier drank 0.465 liters of water in the morning and 0.387 liters of water in the afternoon. How many liters of water did he drink in all?

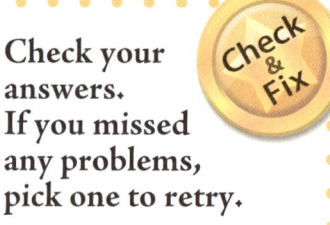

Check your answers. If you missed any problems, pick one to retry.

Ans. _____ liters of water

62

Addition
Up to Thousandths Place
Part One ③

Name

Date

/ /

Score

/ 10

I Add.

(1) 0.256
   + 0.542
   ‾‾‾‾‾‾‾

(4) 0.179
   + 0.372
   ‾‾‾‾‾‾‾

(7) 0.478
   + 0.159
   ‾‾‾‾‾‾‾

(2) 0.392
   + 0.404
   ‾‾‾‾‾‾‾

(5) 0.018
   + 0.228
   ‾‾‾‾‾‾‾

(8) 0.305
   + 0.598
   ‾‾‾‾‾‾‾

(3) 0.298
   + 0.205
   ‾‾‾‾‾‾‾

(6) 0.337
   + 0.514
   ‾‾‾‾‾‾‾

(9) 0.316
   + 0.486
   ‾‾‾‾‾‾‾

2 Alice collected 0.406 gallons of sap from one maple tree. She collected 0.597 gallons of sap from a second maple tree. How many gallons of sap did she collect?

Check your answers. If you missed any problems, pick one to retry.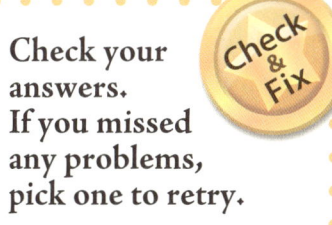

Ans. _____ gallons

63
Addition
Up to Thousandths Place
Part Two ①

Name

Date
/ /

Score
/ 9

1 Add.

(1)
```
   1 . 4 8 5
 + 3 . 9 1 2
 ─────────────
   5 . 3 9 7
```

> Calculate like whole numbers.
> Align the numbers and the decimal points.
> Remember to write the decimal point in your answer.

(2)
```
   2 . 2 1 6
 + 3 . 4 9 1
 ─────────────
```

2 Add.

(1)
```
   4 . 7 2 4
 + 1 . 1 2 7
 ─────────────
```

(3)
```
   3 . 3 7 3
 + 2 . 4 3 1
 ─────────────
```

(5)
```
   4 . 1 9 8
 + 3 . 0 3 4
 ─────────────
```

(2)
```
   4 . 1 9 3
 + 2 . 4 6 8
 ─────────────
```

(4)
```
   7 . 8 0 9
 + 1 . 1 1 2
 ─────────────
```

(6)
```
   5 . 3 8 1
 + 2 . 2 4 5
 ─────────────
```

3 Greg has a bag of grain that weighs 4.193 pounds and a second bag that weighs 2.468 pounds. How much grain does Greg have all together?

Ans. _____ pounds

64 Addition
Up to Thousandths Place
Part Two ②

Name

Date   /   /

Score   / 10

1 Add.

(1)
```
    8 . 8 5 2
  + 1 . 2 7 1
  ─────────────
  1 0 . 1 2 3
```

(2)
```
    5 . 5 6 2
  + 2 . 3 4 9
  ─────────────
```

(3)
```
    7 . 5 4 7
  + 2 . 5 4 7
  ─────────────
```

2 Add.

(1)
```
    1 . 9 4 7
  + 3 . 9 4 2
  ───────────
```

(3)
```
    6 . 1 4 5
  + 2 . 4 5 7
  ───────────
```

(5)
```
    7 . 4 3 9
  + 2 . 6 0 2
  ───────────
```

(2)
```
    4 . 1 2 8
  + 4 . 7 5 7
  ───────────
```

(4)
```
    8 . 3 0 6
  + 2 . 3 4 5
  ───────────
```

(6)
```
    6 . 5 7 8
  + 3 . 4 8 7
  ───────────
```

3 Danica started knitting a scarf and knit 1.485 inches the first day. She knit 3.912 inches the next day. How long is her scarf so far?

Check your answers. If you missed any problems, pick one to retry.

Check & Fix

Ans. _____ inches

65

65

Addition
Up to Thousandths Place
Part Two ③

Name

Date   /   /

Score   /10

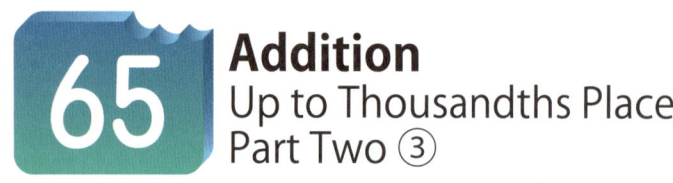

1 Add.

(1)   2.608
    + 4.313
    ⎯⎯⎯⎯

(4)   7.261
    + 1.456
    ⎯⎯⎯⎯

(7)   8.235
    + 2.081
    ⎯⎯⎯⎯

(2)   3.359
    + 5.309
    ⎯⎯⎯⎯

(5)   6.276
    + 2.526
    ⎯⎯⎯⎯

(8)   5.606
    + 4.399
    ⎯⎯⎯⎯

(3)   1.974
    + 2.091
    ⎯⎯⎯⎯

(6)   7.071
    + 1.101
    ⎯⎯⎯⎯

(9)   6.477
    + 3.531
    ⎯⎯⎯⎯

2 Luke is weighing rocks in science class on a scale. The first rock weighs 3.259 grams. The second rock weighs 4.743 grams. If he places both rocks on the scale, what will they weigh together?

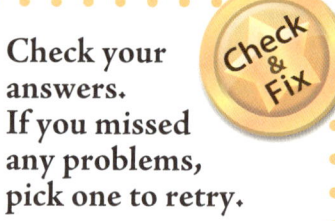

Check your answers. If you missed any problems, pick one to retry.

Ans. _____ grams

Name

Date / /

Score / 9

1 Add.

(1)
```
    3 . 4 7
  + 2 . 7 3
  ─────────
    6 . 2 0
```
6.20 is the same as 6.2.

(2)
```
    0 . 9 6
  + 5 . 0 4
  ─────────
    6 . 0 0
```
6.00 is the same as 6.

2 Add.

(1)
```
    0 . 2 9
  + 2 . 5 1
  ─────────
```

(3)
```
    4 . 5 2
  + 3 . 9 8
  ─────────
```

(5)
```
    6 . 1 6
  + 2 . 8 4
  ─────────
```

(2)
```
    1 . 4 5
  + 3 . 2 5
  ─────────
```

(4)
```
    5 . 3 2
  + 3 . 6 8
  ─────────
```

(6)
```
    2 . 3 1
  + 7 . 6 9
  ─────────
```

3 Nikki collected 4.52 pounds of plastic trash and 3.98 pounds of paper trash from her local park. How many pounds of trash did she collect in total?

Ans. _____ pounds

Addition
The Last Digit
Becomes 0 ②

1 Add.

(1)
```
    8 . 4 3
+   5 . 5 7
```

(2)
```
  1 2 . 9 8
+    7 . 0 2
```

(3)
```
  0 . 5 4 6
+ 0 . 2 5 4
  0 . 8 0̸ 0̸
```

2 Add.

(1)
```
    0 . 1 8
+   3 . 8 2
```

(3)
```
    0 . 1 0 4
+   0 . 6 9 6
```

(5)
```
    0 . 0 2 4
+   0 . 0 7 6
```

(2)
```
    7 . 6 8
+   7 . 3 2
```

(4)
```
    0 . 0 3 2
+   0 . 5 6 8
```

(6)
```
    0 . 8 5 8
+   0 . 0 4 2
```

3 Larry drove his car 0.96 kilometers to the store and then 5.04 kilometers to the post office. How far did he drive in total?

Check your answers.
If you missed any problems, pick one to retry.

Check & Fix

Ans. _____ kilometers

Name

Date

/   /

Score

/10

1 Add.

(1)
```
  0.38
+ 4.12
```

(4)
```
  5.76
+ 4.24
```

(7)
```
  0.297
+ 0.003
```

(2)
```
  4.43
+ 5.47
```

(5)
```
  8.54
+ 4.46
```

(8)
```
  0.335
+ 0.365
```

(3)
```
  5.43
+ 2.57
```

(6)
```
  11.18
+  3.82
```

(9)
```
  0.753
+ 0.147
```

2 Piper has 0.35 yards of pink ribbon and 1.25 yards of yellow ribbon. How much ribbon does she have altogether?

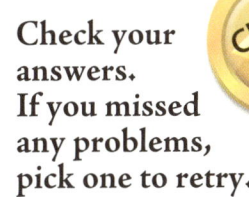

Check your answers. If you missed any problems, pick one to retry.

Ans. _____ yards

69 Addition
Different Digits
Part One ①

Name

Date / /

Score / 9

1 Add.

(1)
```
   2 . 6 3
+  0 . 5 0
─────────
   3 . 1 3
```

> You can write 0.5 as 0.50, then align the numbers and calculate.

(2)
```
   6 . 5 2
+  4 . 0 0
─────────
 1 0 . 5 2
```

2 Add.

(1)
```
  1 . 5 2
+ 1 . 3
─────────
```

(3)
```
  5 . 6 7
+ 2 . 3
─────────
```

(5)
```
  7 . 1 2
+ 3
─────────
```

(2)
```
  2 . 6 3
+ 0 . 5
─────────
```

(4)
```
  3 . 4 7
+ 5
─────────
```

(6)
```
  6 . 5 8
+ 5
─────────
```

3 Elijah bought 2.63 kilograms of white sugar and 0.5 kilograms of brown sugar. How much sugar did he buy in total?

Ans. _____ kilograms

70 **Addition**
Different Digits
Part One ②

Name

Date   /   /

Score

/10

1 Add.

(1)
```
   2 . 4 3 2
 + 1 . 2 2 0
```

(2)
```
   4 . 8 2 5
 + 1 . 4 9 0
```

(3)
```
   0 . 7 1 4
 + 1 . 2 9 0
```

2 Add.

(1)
```
   4 . 3 6 4
 + 3 . 3 5
```

(3)
```
   5 . 0 9 4
 + 3 . 4 1
```

(5)
```
   0 . 6 4 8
 + 1 . 3 8
```

(2)
```
   2 . 6 6 2
 + 3 . 1 4
```

(4)
```
   3 . 8 7 9
 + 2 . 2 1
```

(6)
```
   0 . 3 4 3
 + 1 . 6 6
```

3 Haley biked 4.225 miles one day and 4.13 miles the next day. How many miles did she bike in all?

Check your answers. If you missed any problems, pick one to retry.

Check & Fix

Ans. _____ miles

71

Name

Date / /

Score / 10

1 Add.

(1)   4.31
    + 2.2
    _____

(4)   4.84
    + 6
    _____

(7)   5.638
    + 3.27
    _____

(2)   9.09
    + 0.5
    _____

(5)   7.82
    + 2.2
    _____

(8)   7.793
    + 1.36
    _____

(3)   3.37
    + 2
    _____

(6)   6.181
    + 2.31
    _____

(9)   4.833
    + 3.25
    _____

2 Elliot mixed 1.35 oz of butter and 0.8 oz of sugar. How many ounces of mixture does he have altogether?

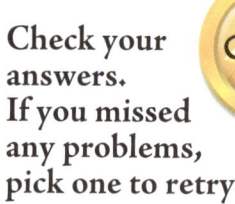

Check your answers. If you missed any problems, pick one to retry.

Ans. _____ oz

Name

Date   /   /

Score   / 9

1 Add.

(1)
```
    1 . 3 0
  + 3 . 9 2
  ─────────
    5 . 2 2
```

> You can write 1.3 as 1.30, then align the numbers and calculate.

(2)
```
    4 . 0 0
  + 3 . 4 2
  ─────────
    7 . 4 2
```

2 Add.

(1)
```
    2 . 5
  + 4 . 3 5
  ─────────
```

(3)
```
    1 . 3
  + 3 . 9 2
  ─────────
```

(5)
```
    5
  + 4 . 2 1
  ─────────
```

(2)
```
    0 . 5
  + 1 . 4 8
  ─────────
```

(4)
```
    3
  + 6 . 7 8
  ─────────
```

(6)
```
    7
  + 3 . 5 5
  ─────────
```

3 Taylor swam 1.3 kilometers to an island in a lake. Then she swam 3.92 kilometers from the island to the other bank of the lake. How far did she swim in total?

Ans. _____ kilometers

Name

Date   /   /

Score
                /10

1 Add.

(1)
```
    3 . 6 0 0
  + 0 . 9 7 4
```

(2)
```
    2 . 2 7 0
  + 1 . 7 6 5
```

(3)
```
    0 . 9 0 0
  + 4 . 4 0 3
```

2 Add.

(1)
```
    3 . 4
  + 0 . 1 3 9
```

(3)
```
    4 . 1 9
  + 3 . 0 1 4
```

(5)
```
    0 . 8
  + 7 . 3 8 7
```

(2)
```
    5 . 4
  + 2 . 4 2 1
```

(4)
```
    0 . 2
  + 5 . 6 0 1
```

(6)
```
    0 . 4
  + 4 . 6 2 3
```

3 Ursula collected 4.5 oz of honey from one of her beehives. She collected 3.425 oz from the second beehive. How much honey did she collect altogether?

Check your answers. If you missed any problems, pick one to retry.

Check & Fix

Ans. _____ oz

Name

Date
/ /

Score
/10

1 Add.

(1)
```
    1.2
 +  5.24
```

(4)
```
    2
 +  7.98
```

(7)
```
    8.65
 +  1.054
```

(2)
```
    0.8
 +  2.31
```

(5)
```
    6
 +  4.33
```

(8)
```
    0.4
 +  8.459
```

(3)
```
    4.2
 +  4.97
```

(6)
```
    4.3
 +  1.578
```

(9)
```
    0.7
 +  6.346
```

2 Emma has 0.4 yards of blue cloth and 1.75 yards of black cloth. How much cloth does she have in all?

Check your answers. If you missed any problems, pick one to retry.

Check & Fix

Ans. _____ yards

75 Addition
Mixed

1 Add.

(1) $\begin{array}{r} 3.6 \\ +\ 1.8 \\ \hline \end{array}$

(2) $\begin{array}{r} 0.96 \\ +\ 3.06 \\ \hline \end{array}$

(3) $\begin{array}{r} 0.67 \\ +\ 0.35 \\ \hline \end{array}$

(4) $\begin{array}{r} 1.95 \\ +\ 4.26 \\ \hline \end{array}$

(5) $\begin{array}{r} 0.425 \\ +\ 0.537 \\ \hline \end{array}$

(6) $\begin{array}{r} 3.168 \\ +\ 3.833 \\ \hline \end{array}$

(7) $\begin{array}{r} 2.63 \\ +\ 2.37 \\ \hline \end{array}$

(8) $\begin{array}{r} 7.87 \\ +\ 0.4 \\ \hline \end{array}$

(9) $\begin{array}{r} 0.8 \\ +\ 4.636 \\ \hline \end{array}$

2 Logan ran 2.5 miles on Tuesday and 3.86 miles on Thursday. How many miles did he run in total?

Ans. _____ miles

Check your answers. If you missed any problems, pick one to retry.

Check & Fix

76

76 Subtraction
Up to Tenths Place ①

1 Subtract.

(1) $1.8 - 0.6 = 1.2$

(2) $4.8 - 1.7 = \boxed{}$

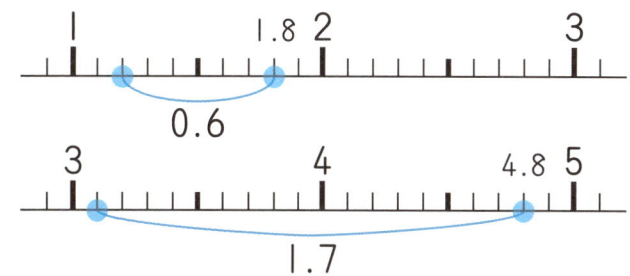

2 Subtract.

(1)
```
    1 . 5
 −  0 . 8
 ────────
    0 . 7
```

(3)
```
    4 . 4
 −  2 . 3
 ────────
```

(5)
```
    8 . 7
 −  3 . 2
 ────────
```

(2)
```
    2 . 7
 −  1 . 2
 ────────
```

(4)
```
    2 . 5
 −  0 . 4
 ────────
```

(6)
```
    2 . 3
 −  0 . 9
 ────────
```

3 Teddy has 2.5 pints of ice cream. He ate 0.4 pints. How much ice cream does he have left?

$2.5 - 0.4 = \boxed{}$

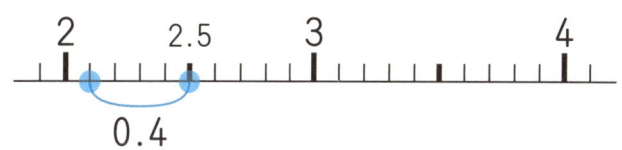

Ans. _____ pints

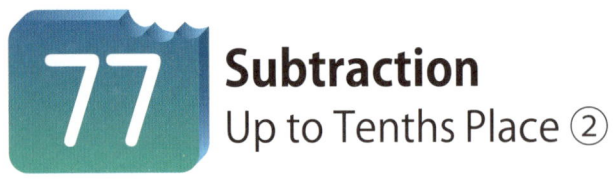
Name

Date

/ /

Score

/ 9

1 Subtract.

(1) $1 - 0.5 =$

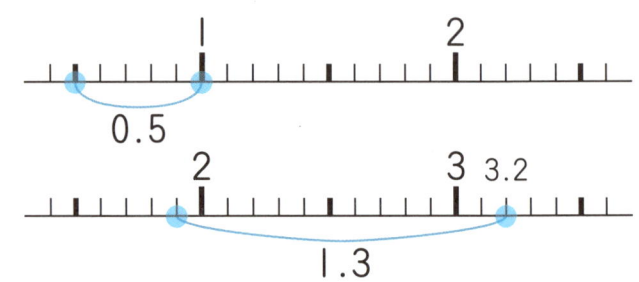

0.5

(2) $3.2 - 1.3 =$

1.3

2 Subtract.

(1)
```
    1
-  0.7
------
   0.3
```

(3)
```
   4.7
-  2.8
------
```

(5)
```
   3.2
-  0.3
------
```

(2)
```
   5.8
-  2.5
------
```

(4)
```
   3.1
-  1
------
```

(6)
```
   4.3
-  0.9
------
```

3 Garret collected 5.6 gallons of rainwater in a month. He used 0.8 gallons to water his plants when it was not raining. How many gallons does he have left?

Check your answers. If you missed any problems, pick one to retry.

Ans. _____ gallons

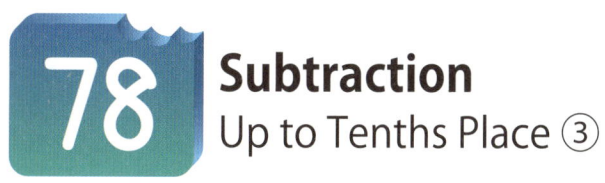

78 Subtraction
Up to Tenths Place ③

Name

Date / /

Score / 11

1 Subtract.

(1) $6.5 - 0.4 =$

(2) $5.3 - 1.5 =$

(3) $1 - 0.2 =$

(4) $4.4 - 1 =$

2 Subtract.

(1)
$$\begin{array}{r} 1.8 \\ -\ 0.5 \\ \hline \end{array}$$

(2)
$$\begin{array}{r} 2.7 \\ -\ 1.2 \\ \hline \end{array}$$

(3)
$$\begin{array}{r} 7.3 \\ -\ 2.7 \\ \hline \end{array}$$

(4)
$$\begin{array}{r} 1 \\ -\ 0.6 \\ \hline \end{array}$$

(5)
$$\begin{array}{r} 1 \\ -\ 0.9 \\ \hline \end{array}$$

(6)
$$\begin{array}{r} 9.8 \\ -\ 1 \\ \hline \end{array}$$

3 June has 1.2 feet of tape. She uses 0.9 feet. How much tape does she have left?

Ans. _____ feet

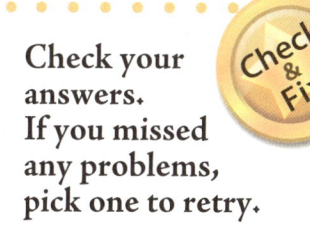

Check your answers.
If you missed any problems, pick one to retry.

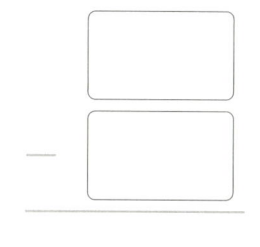

79

79 Subtraction
Up to Hundredths Place
Part One ①

Name

Date
/ /

Score
/ 9

1 Subtract.

(1)
```
    3 . 4 6
  − 2 . 1 8
  ─────────
    1 . 2 8
```

> Calculate like whole numbers.
> Align the numbers and the decimal points.
> Remember to write the decimal point in your answer.

(2)
```
    3 . 4 8
  − 1 . 1 6
  ─────────
```

2 Subtract.

(1)
```
    2 . 4 3
  − 0 . 3 1
  ─────────
```

(3)
```
    5 . 2 6
  − 2 . 2 5
  ─────────
```

(5)
```
    3 . 4 6
  − 2 . 1 8
  ─────────
```

(2)
```
    3 . 5 7
  − 1 . 0 6
  ─────────
```

(4)
```
    8 . 2 6
  − 1 . 1 7
  ─────────
```

(6)
```
    9 . 7 8
  − 0 . 0 9
  ─────────
```

3 Simon measured two feathers in science class. The first feather was 3.46 cm, and the second feather was 2.18 cm. How much longer was the first feather than the second feather?

Ans. _____ cm

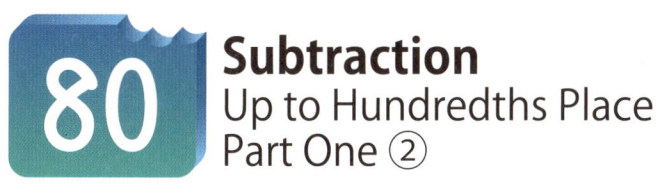

Name

Date   /   /

Score

/10

1 Subtract.

(1)
```
  1 2 . 4 3
-   5 . 1 6
---------
  7 . 2 7
```

(2)
```
  1 4 . 9 9
-   1 . 6 8
---------
```

(3)
```
  2 4 . 5 6
- 1 0 . 2 5
---------
```

2 Subtract.

(1)
```
  1 3 . 5 4
-   2 . 9 1
---------
```

(3)
```
  2 3 . 4 3
- 1 5 . 2 1
---------
```

(5)
```
  2 5 . 4 6
-   9 . 8 1
---------
```

(2)
```
  1 7 . 5 4
-   1 . 8 7
---------
```

(4)
```
  3 0 . 7 3
- 1 2 . 4 8
---------
```

(6)
```
  2 2 . 2 8
- 1 0 . 0 9
---------
```

3 Graham filled a bird feeder with 12.43 grams of bird seed. In one day, the birds ate 5.16 grams. How many grams of seed are left?

Check your answers.
If you missed any problems, pick one to retry.

Check & Fix

Ans. _____ grams

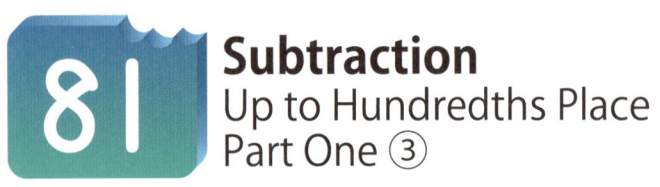

Subtraction
Up to Hundredths Place
Part One ③

Name

Date / /

Score / 10

1 Subtract.

(1)
```
   5.65
−  0.33
```

(4)
```
   8.73
−  0.04
```

(7)
```
  35.16
− 18.27
```

(2)
```
   4.98
−  0.89
```

(5)
```
  11.45
−  1.44
```

(8)
```
  27.63
−  7.16
```

(3)
```
   6.24
−  3.18
```

(6)
```
  18.73
− 12.39
```

(9)
```
  14.48
− 11.85
```

2 Owen bought a piece of wood that was 5.26 inches long. Then, he sawed 1.45 inches off the end. How long is the piece of wood now?

Ans. _____ inches

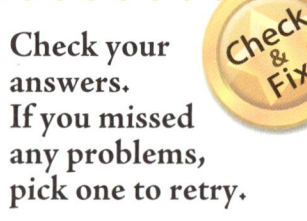

Check your answers. If you missed any problems, pick one to retry.

Name

Date

/ /

Score

/ 9

1 Subtract.

(1)
```
    0 . 7 6
  - 0 . 4 8
  ─────────
    0 . 2 8
```

> Calculate like whole numbers. Align the numbers and the decimal points. Remember to write 0 in the ones column and include the decimal point in your answer.

(2)
```
    1 . 5 6
  - 0 . 9 2
  ─────────
```

2 Subtract.

(1)
```
    5 . 2 1
  - 4 . 3 8
  ─────────
```

(3)
```
    0 . 4 8
  - 0 . 3 3
  ─────────
```

(5)
```
    2 . 7 4
  - 1 . 8 7
  ─────────
```

(2)
```
    2 . 3 7
  - 1 . 6 4
  ─────────
```

(4)
```
    0 . 9 1
  - 0 . 7 4
  ─────────
```

(6)
```
    6 . 4 3
  - 5 . 4 4
  ─────────
```

3 Kyle has 1.56 liters of soda. He pours 0.92 liters for his brother. How much soda does he have left?

Ans. _____ liters

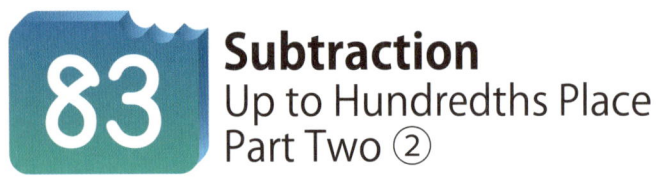

Subtraction
Up to Hundredths Place
Part Two ②

Name

Date
/ /

Score
/ 10

1 Subtract.

(1)
```
  1 0 . 7 3
-     9 . 7 4
-------------
      0 . 9 9
```

(2)
```
  2 . 5 3
- 1 . 7 8
---------
```

(3)
```
  0 . 7 6
- 0 . 4 7
---------
```

2 Subtract.

(1)
```
  0 . 8 3
- 0 . 7 5
---------
```

(3)
```
  7 . 3 7
- 6 . 5 4
---------
```

(5)
```
  1 0 . 2 5
-   9 . 7 1
-----------
```

(2)
```
  4 . 6 7
- 3 . 6 8
---------
```

(4)
```
  1 0 . 3 9
-   9 . 6 6
-----------
```

(6)
```
  8 . 8 4
- 7 . 9 5
---------
```

3 Amy had 9.53 oz of iced tea in her glass. Sam had 8.56 oz of iced tea in her glass. How much more iced tea does Amy have than Sam?

Check your answers. If you missed any problems, pick one to retry.

Check & Fix

Ans. _____ oz

Subtraction
Up to Hundredths Place
Part Two ③

Name

Date   /   /

Score

/ 10

1 Subtract.

(1)
```
   6.47
 - 5.56
```

(4)
```
   7.18
 - 6.56
```

(7)
```
  10.74
 - 9.95
```

(2)
```
   0.93
 - 0.72
```

(5)
```
   9.03
 - 8.75
```

(8)
```
  10.16
 - 9.24
```

(3)
```
   5.64
 - 5.56
```

(6)
```
   6.37
 - 5.54
```

(9)
```
  10.13
 - 9.42
```

2 Chloe has 2.74 pounds of soil. She used 2.56 pounds to plant tulips. How much soil does she have left?

Check your answers. If you missed any problems, pick one to retry.

Check & Fix

Ans. _____ pounds

85 Subtraction
Up to Thousandths Place
Part One ①

Name

Date
    /   /

Score
    / 9

1 Subtract.

(1)
```
    6 . 2 4 1
  − 2 . 1 5 3
  ───────────
    4 . 0 8 8
```

> Calculate like whole numbers.
> Align the numbers and the decimal points.
> Remember to write the decimal point in your answer.

(2)
```
    2 . 8 1 6
  − 1 . 5 2 1
  ───────────
```

2 Subtract.

(1)
```
    8 . 0 2 5
  − 3 . 1 7 4
  ───────────
```

(3)
```
    4 . 1 6 7
  − 1 . 2 5 5
  ───────────
```

(5)
```
    5 . 9 2 2
  − 3 . 6 7 1
  ───────────
```

(2)
```
    3 . 1 5 2
  − 0 . 5 4 1
  ───────────
```

(4)
```
    6 . 2 6 5
  − 2 . 2 1 3
  ───────────
```

(6)
```
    3 . 4 7 1
  − 0 . 6 6 2
  ───────────
```

3 Wayne drove 3.152 miles on Monday and 0.541 miles on Tuesday. How many more miles did he drive on Monday than on Tuesday?

Ans.   miles

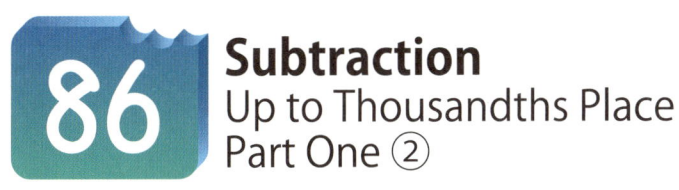
Name

Date
/ /

Score
/10

1 Subtract.

(1)
```
  5 . 0 0 4
− 1 . 2 3 6
```

(2)
```
  6 . 0 1 6
− 4 . 0 9 8
```

(3)
```
  7 . 4 1 3
− 5 . 0 1 2
```

2 Subtract.

(1)
```
  2 . 8 1 8
− 1 . 3 3 4
```

(3)
```
  4 . 3 4 6
− 2 . 0 8 3
```

(5)
```
  8 . 1 7 9
− 3 . 8 0 5
```

(2)
```
  6 . 2 9 6
− 0 . 5 7 2
```

(4)
```
  1 . 0 7 1
− 0 . 0 6 3
```

(6)
```
  5 . 6 3 1
− 3 . 8 0 2
```

3 Penelope bought 9.103 kilograms of hay to feed her horses. She gives them 4.098 kilograms in the morning. How many kilograms of hay does she have left?

Check your answers. If you missed any problems, pick one to retry.

Check & Fix

Ans. _____ kilograms

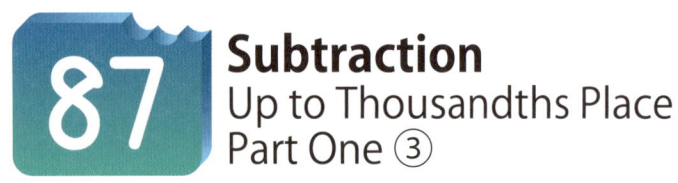

Subtraction
Up to Thousandths Place
Part One ③

Name

Date   /   /

Score   / 10

1 Subtract.

(1)   4.619
    − 2.786
    _____

(2)   7.432
    − 3.364
    _____

(3)   5.469
    − 1.821
    _____

(4)   9.171
    − 4.432
    _____

(5)   6.804
    − 2.127
    _____

(6)   5.588
    − 2.661
    _____

(7)   4.058
    − 1.987
    _____

(8)   1.739
    − 0.608
    _____

(9)   7.361
    − 0.702
    _____

2 Wyatt has 8.209 liters of water. He uses 4.163 liters to make lemonade for a party. How much water does he have left?

Check your answers. If you missed any problems, pick one to retry.

Check & Fix

Ans. _____   liters

Subtraction
Up to Thousandths Place
Part Two ①

Name

Date

/ /

Score

/ 9

1 Subtract.

(1)
```
    5 . 7 6 3
  − 5 . 1 4 2
  ─────────
    0 . 6 2 1
```

> Calculate like whole numbers.
> Align the numbers and the decimal points.
> Remember to write 0 in the ones column and include the decimal point in your answer.

(2)
```
    1 . 5 4 6
  − 0 . 7 4 2
  ─────────
```

2 Subtract.

(1)
```
    2 . 5 4 8
  − 1 . 7 3 3
  ─────────
```

(3)
```
    5 . 7 6 3
  − 5 . 1 4 2
  ─────────
```

(5)
```
    4 . 2 7 1
  − 3 . 4 0 7
  ─────────
```

(2)
```
    3 . 2 5 3
  − 3 . 0 5 5
  ─────────
```

(4)
```
    1 . 4 1 5
  − 0 . 8 2 9
  ─────────
```

(6)
```
    1 . 8 3 8
  − 0 . 9 1 6
  ─────────
```

3 Kelly planted 5.763 meters of corn and 5.142 meters of wheat. How many more meters of corn did she plant than wheat?

Ans. _____ meters

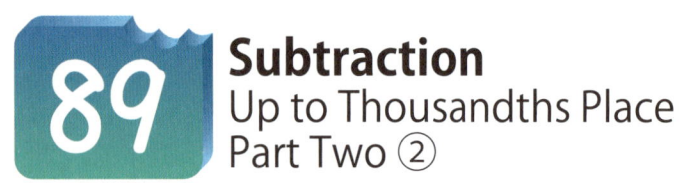

Subtraction
Up to Thousandths Place
Part Two ②

Name

Date
/ /

Score
/ 10

1 Subtract.

(1)
```
  0.416
- 0.175
```

(2)
```
  0.773
- 0.499
```

(3)
```
  2.286
- 1.393
```

2 Subtract.

(1)
```
  0.534
- 0.232
```

(3)
```
  0.384
- 0.047
```

(5)
```
  8.028
- 7.379
```

(2)
```
  4.385
- 4.242
```

(4)
```
  5.225
- 4.311
```

(6)
```
  0.827
- 0.631
```

3 Isaac is measuring leaves for a science project. The first leaf is 4.705 inches, and the second leaf is 3.762 inches. What is the difference between the two leaves?

Check your answers. If you missed any problems, pick one to retry.

Check & Fix

Ans. _____ inches

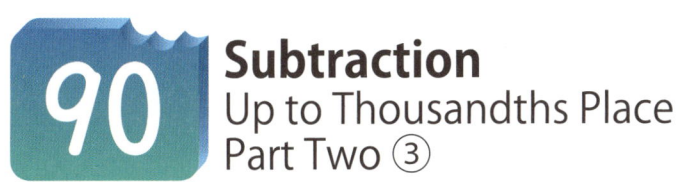

90 Subtraction
Up to Thousandths Place
Part Two ③

Name _____

Date ___/___/___

Score ___/10

1 Subtract.

(1)
```
   0.339
 - 0.163
```

(4)
```
   0.821
 - 0.388
```

(7)
```
   6.587
 - 5.856
```

(2)
```
   6.993
 - 6.841
```

(5)
```
   7.258
 - 6.885
```

(8)
```
   8.812
 - 8.553
```

(3)
```
   5.337
 - 5.118
```

(6)
```
   9.429
 - 9.143
```

(9)
```
   4.058
 - 3.637
```

2 Stephanie weighed two bags of oranges in the supermarket. One bag weighed 6.251 pounds and the other bag weighed 5.634 pounds. What is the difference in weight between the two bags of oranges?

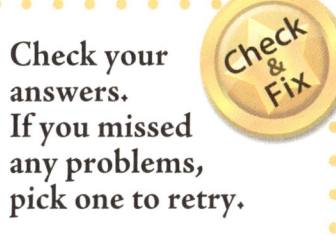

Check your answers.
If you missed any problems, pick one to retry.

Ans. _____ pounds

Name

Date
/ /

Score
/ 9

1 Subtract.

(1)
```
    4 . 3 4
  − 2 . 9 4
  ─────────
    1 . 4 0
```
1.40 is the same as 1.4.

(2)
```
  1 2 . 6 4
  −   8 . 6 4
  ───────────
    4 . 0 0
```
4.00 is the same as 4.

2 Subtract.

(1)
```
    5 . 2 9
  − 2 . 1 9
  ─────────
```

(3)
```
  1 4 . 3
  −   6 . 3
  ─────────
```

(5)
```
  1 6 . 1 6
  −   6 . 1 6
  ───────────
```

(2)
```
    4 . 3 4
  − 2 . 9 4
  ─────────
```

(4)
```
  1 5 . 4 3
  −   3 . 4 3
  ───────────
```

(6)
```
  1 3 . 3 1
  −   7 . 3 1
  ───────────
```

3 Quinn bought 4.34 yards of rope to hang some plant baskets. She uses 2.94 yards. How many yards of rope does she have left?

Ans. _____ yards

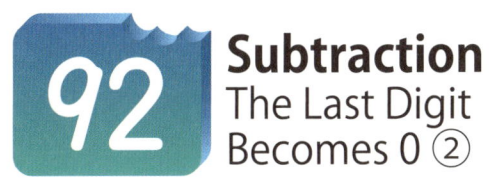

Subtraction
The Last Digit
Becomes 0 ②

Name

Date
/ /

Score
/ 10

1 Subtract.

(1)
```
    9 . 4 1 6
 -  3 . 8 1 6
 -----------
    5 . 6 0 0
```

(2)
```
    3 . 5 7 6
 -  2 . 1 4 6
 -----------
```

(3)
```
    0 . 7 2 7
 -  0 . 6 5 7
 -----------
    0 . 0 7 0
```

2 Subtract.

(1)
```
    3.656
 -  2.156
 --------
```

(3)
```
    6.267
 -  4.157
 --------
```

(5)
```
    0.698
 -  0.638
 --------
```

(2)
```
   14.87
 -  4.87
 -------
```

(4)
```
    4.373
 -  2.183
 --------
```

(6)
```
    0.254
 -  0.164
 --------
```

3 Colleen bought 12.64 cm of tape for a project. She used 8.64 cm. How much tape does she have left?

Check your answers. If you missed any problems, pick one to retry.

Check & Fix

Ans. _____ cm

93

Subtraction
The Last Digit Becomes 0 ③

Name

Date   /   /

Score   /10

1 Subtract.

(1)
```
    4.28
  − 3.18
  _____
```

(4)
```
   18.34
  −  6.44
  _____
```

(7)
```
    7.417
  − 2.717
  _____
```

(2)
```
    15.6
  −  5.6
  _____
```

(5)
```
    6.314
  − 3.114
  _____
```

(8)
```
    6.34
  − 3.54
  _____
```

(3)
```
   24.35
  −  7.35
  _____
```

(6)
```
    8.973
  − 2.193
  _____
```

(9)
```
    8.74
  − 2.74
  _____
```

2 Carter has 2.35 kilograms of clay. He used 0.75 kilograms to make a large bowl. How much clay does he have left?

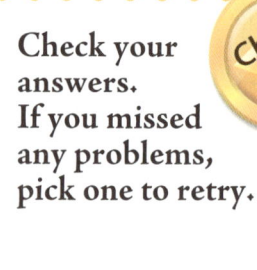

Check your answers. If you missed any problems, pick one to retry.

Ans. _____ kilograms

94 **Subtraction**
Different Digits
Part One ①

Name

Date
/ /

Score
/ 9

1 Subtract.

(1)
```
  8 . 2 4
- 5 . 9 0
---------
  2 . 3 4
```

> You can write 5.9 as 5.90, then align the numbers and calculate.

(2)
```
  5 . 4 3
- 2 . 1 0
---------
```

2 Subtract.

(1)
```
  4 . 5 3
- 3 . 1
---------
```

(3)
```
  8 . 2 4
- 5 . 9
---------
```

(5)
```
  7 . 7 6
- 5 . 8
---------
```

(2)
```
  6 . 7 3
- 4 . 6
---------
```

(4)
```
  8 . 5 1
- 4 . 7
---------
```

(6)
```
  3 . 4 8
- 1 . 8
---------
```

3 Derek collected 8.24 pounds of trash. He was able to recycle 5.9 pounds. How much trash does he have left to throw away?

Ans. _____ pounds

95

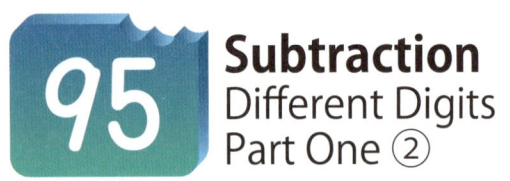

Name

Date
    /   /

Score
    / 10

1 Subtract.

(1)
```
  0.903
- 0.720
```

(2)
```
  8.241
- 4.360
```

(3)
```
  12.09
-  6.70
```

2 Subtract.

(1)
```
  0.352
- 0.21
```

(3)
```
  6.657
- 2.31
```

(5)
```
  10.83
-  4.6
```

(2)
```
  0.678
- 0.49
```

(4)
```
  8.434
- 4.18
```

(6)
```
  16.32
-  5.9
```

3 Zane bought 12.09 oz of cheese for a party. His friends ate 6.7 oz. How much cheese does he have left?

Check your answers. If you missed any problems, pick one to retry.

Check & Fix

Ans. _____ oz

Name

Date

/ /

Score

/ 10

1 Subtract.

(1)
```
   3.49
 − 1.1
```

(4)
```
   0.561
 − 0.23
```

(7)
```
   7.617
 − 5.23
```

(2)
```
   7.83
 − 3.9
```

(5)
```
   0.747
 − 0.28
```

(8)
```
   11.62
 −  5.1
```

(3)
```
   4.62
 − 2.8
```

(6)
```
   8.644
 − 4.14
```

(9)
```
   13.45
 −  7.7
```

2 Hazel picked 3.52 pounds of blueberries and 1.6 pounds of raspberries. How many more pounds of blueberries did she pick than raspberries?

Check your
answers.
If you missed
any problems,
pick one to retry.

Check
&
Fix

Ans. _____ pounds

Name

Date

/ /

Score

/ 9

1 Subtract.

(1)
```
    3 . 2 0
  - 1 . 5 6
  ─────────
    1 . 6 4
```

3.2 is the same as 3.20.

(2)
```
    4 . 0 0
  - 1 . 4 2
  ─────────
    2 . 5 8
```

2 Subtract.

(1)
```
    3 . 5
  - 2 . 1 4
  ─────────
```

(3)
```
  1 8 . 4
  -  4 . 2 2
  ─────────
```

(5)
```
    5
  - 1 . 4 8
  ─────────
```

(2)
```
    6 . 1
  - 3 . 4 3
  ─────────
```

(4)
```
    7
  - 3 . 1 6
  ─────────
```

(6)
```
  1 8
  -  2 . 6 3
  ─────────
```

3 The hedge in Alex's yard is 6.1 feet tall. He cuts 3.43 feet off the top of the hedge. How tall is the hedge now?

Ans. _____ feet

Name

Date   /   /

Score   /10

1 Subtract.

(1)
```
   2 . 6 4 0
 - 1 . 8 1 5
```

(2)
```
   2 . 7 0 0
 - 0 . 9 5 3
```

(3)
```
   1 . 0 0 0
 - 0 . 8 8 3
```

2 Subtract.

(1)
```
   3 . 4 8
 - 2 . 3 4 1
```

(3)
```
   4 . 5
 - 0 . 4 4 6
```

(5)
```
   1
 - 0 . 2 6 9
```

(2)
```
   9 . 7 7
 - 4 . 8 3 4
```

(4)
```
   8 . 8
 - 1 . 2 5 5
```

(6)
```
   5
 - 3 . 1 1 6
```

3 Francis made 7 quarts of lemonade for her lemonade stand. She sold 3.315 quarts. How much lemonade does she have left?

Check your answers. If you missed any problems, pick one to retry.

Check & Fix

Ans. _____ quarts

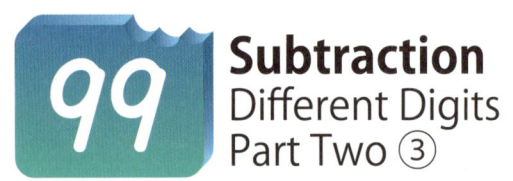

Subtraction
Different Digits
Part Two ③

Name _____

Date _____/_____/_____

Score _____/10

1 Subtract.

(1)
```
   4 . 2
-  1 . 1 2
```

(4)
```
   8 . 5 4
-  3 . 7 2 5
```

(7)
```
   4 . 1
-  1 . 1 7 4
```

(2)
```
  2 3 . 5
-    6 . 3 3
```

(5)
```
   7 . 5 3
-  5 . 4 8 1
```

(8)
```
   1
-  0 . 4 3 6
```

(3)
```
  1 7
-    5 . 6 8
```

(6)
```
   6 . 7
-  0 . 3 2 8
```

(9)
```
   8
-  6 . 2 6 8
```

2 David has 3.2 liters of broth. He uses 0.89 liters to make soup. How many liters does he have left?

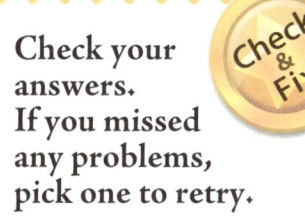

Check your answers. If you missed any problems, pick one to retry.

Check & Fix

Ans. _____ liters

100 Subtraction
Mixed

Name _____

Date ___/___/___

Score ___/10

1 Subtract.

(1)
```
    6.3
  - 3.8
  _____
```

(4)
```
   0.57
 - 0.28
 _____
```

(7)
```
   8.226
 - 3.016
 _____
```

(2)
```
   19.36
 -  6.15
 _____
```

(5)
```
   6.748
 - 4.309
 _____
```

(8)
```
   9
 - 7.23
 _____
```

(3)
```
   8.72
 - 4.15
 _____
```

(6)
```
   6.894
 - 5.973
 _____
```

(9)
```
   1
 - 0.528
 _____
```

2 Lola has 4 feet of wrapping paper. She uses 2.45 feet to wrap a present. How much does she have left?

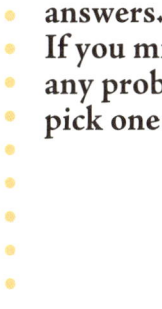

Check your answers. If you missed any problems, pick one to retry.

Check & Fix

Ans. _____ feet

101

MathBites
Fractions & Decimals Grade 4

Answer Key

---

1 Introduction
Review ① p.2

1 (1) > (2) < (3) =

2 (1) > (2) < (3) > (4) =

---

2 Introduction
Review ② p.3

1 (1) $2\frac{3}{4}$ (2) 3 (3) $2\frac{1}{6}$ (4) 3

---

3 Addition
Proper Fractions: Part One ① p.4

1 (1) $\frac{2}{5}$ (2) $\frac{3}{4}$ (3) $\frac{2}{3}$ (4) $\frac{5}{6}$ (5) $\frac{3}{7}$

2 (1) $\frac{3}{5}$ (2) $\frac{5}{6}$ (3) $\frac{6}{7}$ (4) $\frac{5}{8}$

3 $\frac{1}{3} + \frac{1}{3} = \frac{2}{3}$ Ans. $\frac{2}{3}$ of a mile

---

4 Addition
Proper Fractions: Part One ② p.5

1 (1) $\frac{3}{4}$ (2) $\frac{5}{7}$ (3) $\frac{3}{8}$ (4) $\frac{5}{9}$

2 (1) $\frac{5}{6}$ (2) $\frac{4}{9}$ (3) $\frac{7}{10}$ (4) $\frac{6}{7}$

3 $\frac{3}{7} + \frac{1}{7} = \frac{4}{7}$ Ans. $\frac{4}{7}$ of the can of paint

---

5 Addition
Proper Fractions: Part One ③ p.6

1 (1) $\frac{4}{5}$ (3) $\frac{7}{10}$ (5) $\frac{4}{7}$ (7) $\frac{9}{10}$
(2) $\frac{7}{8}$ (4) $\frac{7}{9}$ (6) $\frac{4}{5}$ (8) $\frac{8}{9}$

2 $\frac{2}{5} + \frac{1}{5} = \frac{3}{5}$ Ans. $\frac{3}{5}$ of a liter of juice

---

6 Addition
Proper Fractions: Part Two ① p.7

1 $\frac{6}{5}$, $1\frac{1}{5}$

2 (1) $\frac{5}{4}$, $1\frac{1}{4}$ (2) $\frac{5}{3}$, $1\frac{2}{3}$ (3) $1\frac{1}{6}$ (4) $1\frac{2}{7}$

3 $\frac{2}{3} + \frac{2}{3} = \frac{4}{3} = 1\frac{1}{3}$ Ans. $1\frac{1}{3}$ yards

---

7 Addition
Proper Fractions: Part Two ② p.8

1 (1) $\frac{8}{7}$, $1\frac{1}{7}$ (2) $\frac{6}{6}$, 1

2 (1) $1\frac{2}{5}$ (2) $1\frac{1}{8}$ (3) 1 (4) 1

3 $\frac{1}{6} + \frac{5}{6} = \frac{6}{6} = 1$ Ans. 1 mile

---

8 Addition
Proper Fractions: Part Two ③ p.9

1 (1) $1\frac{1}{4}$ (3) $1\frac{2}{9}$ (5) 1
(2) 1 (4) $1\frac{3}{8}$ (6) $1\frac{3}{7}$

2 $\frac{2}{8} + \frac{7}{8} = \frac{9}{8} = 1\frac{1}{8}$ Ans. $1\frac{1}{8}$ laps

9 Addition
Improper Fractions ① p.10

1 $\dfrac{11}{4}$, $2\dfrac{3}{4}$

2 (1) $\dfrac{8}{3}$, $2\dfrac{2}{3}$ (2) $\dfrac{12}{5}$, $2\dfrac{2}{5}$ (3) $1\dfrac{5}{6}$ (4) $2\dfrac{1}{4}$

3 $\dfrac{3}{5}+\dfrac{9}{5}=\dfrac{12}{5}=2\dfrac{2}{5}$ Ans. $2\dfrac{2}{5}$ buckets of seashells

10 Addition
Improper Fractions ② p.11

1 (1) $\dfrac{13}{3}$, $4\dfrac{1}{3}$ (2) $\dfrac{13}{4}$, $3\dfrac{1}{4}$

2 (1) $2\dfrac{3}{5}$ (2) $2\dfrac{1}{6}$ (3) $3\dfrac{1}{4}$ (4) $3\dfrac{1}{3}$

3 $\dfrac{3}{2}+\dfrac{1}{2}=\dfrac{4}{2}=2$ Ans. 2 cups

11 Addition
Improper Fractions ③ p.12

1 (1) $1\dfrac{3}{5}$ (3) $3\dfrac{1}{4}$ (5) $2\dfrac{2}{7}$
(2) $1\dfrac{4}{9}$ (4) 2 (6) $3\dfrac{1}{5}$

2 $\dfrac{9}{4}+\dfrac{6}{4}=\dfrac{15}{4}=3\dfrac{3}{4}$ Ans. $3\dfrac{3}{4}$ teaspoons

12 Addition
Mixed Numbers: Part One ① p.13

1 (1) $3\dfrac{5}{6}$ (2) $3\dfrac{5}{8}$ (3) $3\dfrac{2}{3}$ (4) $2\dfrac{3}{10}$

2 (1) $4\dfrac{2}{5}$ (2) $2\dfrac{1}{6}$ (3) $3\dfrac{3}{4}$ (4) $4\dfrac{1}{9}$

3 $2\dfrac{3}{4}+1=3\dfrac{3}{4}$ Ans. $3\dfrac{3}{4}$ cups

13 Addition
Mixed Numbers: Part One ② p.14

1 (1) $3\dfrac{3}{4}$ (2) $4\dfrac{3}{5}$

2 (1) $5\dfrac{3}{7}$ (2) $4\dfrac{4}{9}$ (3) $4\dfrac{1}{6}$ (4) $2\dfrac{7}{10}$

3 $3+\dfrac{3}{10}=3\dfrac{3}{10}$ Ans. $3\dfrac{3}{10}$ miles

14 Addition
Mixed Numbers: Part One ③ p.15

1 (1) $4\dfrac{1}{2}$ (3) $3\dfrac{5}{6}$ (5) $3\dfrac{5}{9}$ (7) $4\dfrac{3}{4}$
(2) $4\dfrac{4}{5}$ (4) $3\dfrac{9}{10}$ (6) $3\dfrac{7}{8}$ (8) $4\dfrac{2}{7}$

2 $2+2\dfrac{4}{7}=4\dfrac{4}{7}$ Ans. $4\dfrac{4}{7}$ bags of food

15 Addition
Mixed Numbers: Part Two ① p.16

1 (1) $1\dfrac{4}{5}$ (2) $2\dfrac{4}{7}$ (3) $2\dfrac{7}{10}$ (4) $1\dfrac{5}{6}$

2 (1) $2\dfrac{6}{7}$ (2) $3\dfrac{2}{3}$ (3) $1\dfrac{5}{8}$ (4) $2\dfrac{3}{4}$

3 $2\dfrac{4}{7}+\dfrac{2}{7}=2\dfrac{6}{7}$ Ans. $2\dfrac{6}{7}$ boxes

16 Addition
Mixed Numbers: Part Two ② p.17

1 (1) $3\dfrac{3}{4}$ (2) $2\dfrac{5}{7}$

2 (1) $2\dfrac{4}{5}$ (2) $2\dfrac{7}{8}$ (3) $1\dfrac{9}{10}$ (4) $3\dfrac{5}{9}$

3 $1\dfrac{2}{8}+\dfrac{5}{8}=1\dfrac{7}{8}$ Ans. $1\dfrac{7}{8}$ balls of yarn

17 Addition
Mixed Numbers: Part Three ① p.18

1 $1\dfrac{7}{5}$, $2\dfrac{2}{5}$

2 (1) $1\dfrac{4}{3}$, $2\dfrac{1}{3}$ (2) $3\dfrac{1}{6}$ (3) $2\dfrac{2}{9}$ (4) $3\dfrac{1}{5}$

3 $\dfrac{2}{6}+2\dfrac{5}{6}=2\dfrac{7}{6}=3\dfrac{1}{6}$ Ans. $3\dfrac{1}{6}$ hours

18 Addition
Mixed Numbers: Part Three ② p.19

1 (1) $2\dfrac{5}{4}$, $3\dfrac{1}{4}$ (2) $3\dfrac{9}{7}$, $4\dfrac{2}{7}$

2 (1) $3\dfrac{1}{5}$ (2) $2\dfrac{2}{9}$ (3) $3\dfrac{1}{7}$ (4) $4\dfrac{3}{8}$

3 $\dfrac{3}{5}+1\dfrac{4}{5}=1\dfrac{7}{5}=2\dfrac{2}{5}$ Ans. $2\dfrac{2}{5}$ miles

19 Addition
Mixed Numbers: Part Four ① p.20

1 (1) $3\frac{2}{3}$ (2) $4\frac{3}{5}$ (3) $4\frac{6}{7}$ (4) $4\frac{3}{4}$

2 (1) $3\frac{5}{6}$ (2) $3\frac{3}{4}$ (3) $3\frac{5}{8}$ (4) $3\frac{4}{5}$

3 $1\frac{1}{4}+2\frac{2}{4}=3\frac{3}{4}$ Ans. $3\frac{3}{4}$ bags

20 Addition
Mixed Numbers: Part Four ② p.21

1 (1) $4\frac{5}{6}$ (2) $5\frac{3}{8}$

2 (1) $5\frac{3}{4}$ (2) $4\frac{4}{9}$ (3) $4\frac{3}{5}$ (4) $5\frac{7}{10}$

3 $2\frac{2}{9}+3\frac{5}{9}=5\frac{7}{9}$ Ans. $5\frac{7}{9}$ books

21 Addition
Mixed Numbers: Part Five ① p.22

1 $3\frac{4}{3}$, $4\frac{1}{3}$

2 (1) $3\frac{7}{5}$, $4\frac{2}{5}$ (2) $4\frac{3}{4}$ (3) $4\frac{2}{7}$ (4) $3\frac{1}{6}$

3 $2\frac{4}{5}+1\frac{3}{5}=3\frac{7}{5}=4\frac{2}{5}$ Ans. $4\frac{2}{5}$ miles

22 Addition
Mixed Numbers: Part Five ② p.23

1 (1) $3\frac{5}{4}$, $4\frac{1}{4}$ (2) $4\frac{7}{5}$, $5\frac{2}{5}$

2 (1) $4\frac{1}{7}$ (2) $4\frac{2}{9}$ (3) $5\frac{3}{5}$ (4) $3\frac{1}{8}$

3 $1\frac{3}{6}+3\frac{4}{6}=4\frac{7}{6}=5\frac{1}{6}$ Ans. $5\frac{1}{6}$ inches

23 Addition
The Answer Becomes a Whole Number ① p.24

1 $4\frac{3}{3}$, 5

2 (1) $1\frac{6}{6}$, 2 (2) 5 (3) 3 (4) 4

3 $2\frac{5}{7}+2\frac{2}{7}=4\frac{7}{7}=5$ Ans. 5 kilograms

24 Addition
The Answer Becomes a Whole Number ② p.25

1 (1) $2\frac{5}{5}$, 3 (2) $4\frac{6}{6}$, 5

2 (1) 3 (2) 4 (3) 5 (4) 4

3 $3\frac{5}{8}+1\frac{3}{8}=4\frac{8}{8}=5$ Ans. 5 packs of paper

25 Addition
Mixed p.26

1 (1) $\frac{5}{7}$ (3) $2\frac{3}{4}$ (5) $5\frac{1}{6}$
(2) $1\frac{2}{5}$ (4) $3\frac{5}{8}$ (6) 4

2 $1\frac{3}{5}+1\frac{4}{5}=2\frac{7}{5}=3\frac{2}{5}$ Ans. $3\frac{2}{5}$ cm

26 Subtraction
Proper Fractions ① p.27

1 (1) $\frac{2}{5}$ (2) $\frac{1}{4}$ (3) $\frac{1}{3}$ (4) $\frac{1}{6}$ (5) $\frac{3}{7}$

2 (1) $\frac{2}{5}$ (2) $\frac{1}{6}$ (3) $\frac{1}{4}$ (4) $\frac{3}{5}$

3 $\frac{2}{3}-\frac{1}{3}=\frac{1}{3}$ Ans. $\frac{1}{3}$ of a cup

27 Subtraction
Proper Fractions ② p.28

1 (1) $\frac{1}{6}$ (2) $\frac{3}{7}$ (3) $\frac{3}{8}$ (4) $\frac{2}{9}$

2 (1) $\frac{2}{7}$ (2) $\frac{2}{9}$ (3) $\frac{1}{10}$ (4) $\frac{3}{7}$

3 $\frac{7}{10}-\frac{4}{10}=\frac{3}{10}$ Ans. $\frac{3}{10}$ of a yard

28 Subtraction
Proper Fractions ③ p.29

1 (1) $\frac{1}{4}$ (3) $\frac{1}{9}$ (5) $\frac{1}{5}$ (7) $\frac{1}{8}$
(2) $\frac{1}{6}$ (4) $\frac{2}{7}$ (6) $\frac{3}{10}$ (8) $\frac{2}{9}$

2 $\frac{6}{8}-\frac{3}{8}=\frac{3}{8}$ Ans. $\frac{3}{8}$ of a yard

29 Subtraction
Improper Fractions ① p.30

1. $\frac{4}{3}$, $1\frac{1}{3}$

2. (1) $\frac{1}{3}$ (2) $\frac{6}{5}$, $1\frac{1}{5}$ (3) $\frac{4}{7}$ (4) $1\frac{1}{6}$

3. $\frac{12}{5} - \frac{6}{5} = \frac{6}{5} = 1\frac{1}{5}$ Ans. $1\frac{1}{5}$ ml

30 Subtraction
Improper Fractions ② p.31

1. (1) $\frac{7}{4}$, $1\frac{3}{4}$ (2) $\frac{6}{3}$, 2

2. (1) $1\frac{2}{5}$ (2) 1 (3) 2 (4) $2\frac{1}{4}$

3. $\frac{8}{3} - \frac{1}{3} = \frac{7}{3} = 2\frac{1}{3}$ Ans. $2\frac{1}{3}$ loaves

31 Subtraction
Improper Fractions ③ p.32

1. (1) $1\frac{3}{5}$ (3) $2\frac{1}{2}$ (5) 1
   (2) 2 (4) $1\frac{1}{6}$ (6) $2\frac{2}{3}$

2. $\frac{13}{6} - \frac{7}{6} = \frac{6}{6} = 1$ Ans. 1 pound

32 Subtraction
Mixed Numbers: Part One ① p.33

1. (1) $1\frac{1}{4}$ (2) $1\frac{2}{3}$ (3) $1\frac{3}{4}$ (4) $\frac{3}{5}$ (5) $\frac{5}{6}$

2. (1) $1\frac{3}{8}$ (2) $2\frac{2}{7}$ (3) $\frac{1}{6}$ (4) $\frac{4}{9}$

3. $3\frac{1}{4} - 2 = 1\frac{1}{4}$ Ans. $1\frac{1}{4}$ pints

33 Subtraction
Mixed Numbers: Part One ② p.34

1. (1) $1\frac{1}{2}$ (3) $\frac{1}{6}$ (5) $2\frac{6}{7}$ (7) $\frac{3}{8}$
   (2) $\frac{2}{3}$ (4) $2\frac{2}{5}$ (6) $\frac{3}{4}$ (8) $1\frac{7}{9}$

2. $2\frac{4}{5} - 2 = \frac{4}{5}$ Ans. $\frac{4}{5}$ of a cup

34 Subtraction
Mixed Numbers: Part Two ① p.35

1. (1) $1\frac{2}{5}$ (2) $2\frac{1}{4}$ (3) 4

2. (1) $3\frac{1}{6}$ (2) $2\frac{1}{9}$ (3) 3 (4) 2

3. $2\frac{4}{9} - \frac{3}{9} = 2\frac{1}{9}$ Ans. $2\frac{1}{9}$ hours

35 Subtraction
Mixed Numbers: Part Two ② p.36

1. (1) $1\frac{3}{7}$ (2) 3

2. (1) 1 (2) $4\frac{1}{6}$ (3) $1\frac{3}{10}$ (4) 3

3. $2\frac{6}{8} - \frac{3}{8} = 2\frac{3}{8}$ Ans. $2\frac{3}{8}$ pounds

36 Subtraction
Mixed Numbers: Part Three ① p.37

1. $\frac{5}{4}$, $\frac{3}{4}$

2. (1) $\frac{7}{5}$, $\frac{4}{5}$ (2) $\frac{10}{6}$, $\frac{5}{6}$ (3) $\frac{4}{9}$ (4) $\frac{5}{8}$

3. $1\frac{4}{6} - \frac{5}{6} = \frac{10}{6} - \frac{5}{6}$
   $= \frac{5}{6}$ Ans. $\frac{5}{6}$ of a foot

37 Subtraction
Mixed Numbers: Part Three ② p.38

1 (1) $1\frac{4}{3}$, $1\frac{2}{3}$ (2) $2\frac{8}{5}$, $2\frac{4}{5}$

2 (1) $2\frac{8}{6}$, $2\frac{5}{6}$ (2) $3\frac{6}{7}$ (3) $1\frac{7}{10}$ (4) $2\frac{3}{4}$

3 $4\frac{1}{5} - \frac{4}{5} = 3\frac{6}{5} - \frac{4}{5}$

$= 3\frac{2}{5}$ Ans. $3\frac{2}{5}$ grams of candy

38 Subtraction
Mixed Numbers: Part Four ① p.39

1 (1) $3\frac{1}{3}$ (2) $\frac{2}{5}$ (3) 2

2 (1) $2\frac{1}{6}$ (2) $1\frac{4}{7}$ (3) $\frac{1}{6}$ (4) 1

3 $3\frac{4}{6} - 1\frac{3}{6} = 2\frac{1}{6}$ Ans. $2\frac{1}{6}$ hours

39 Subtraction
Mixed Numbers: Part Four ② p.40

1 (1) $1\frac{5}{8}$ (2) $\frac{2}{9}$

2 (1) 2 (2) $\frac{1}{6}$ (3) $2\frac{1}{5}$ (4) $3\frac{1}{4}$

3 $4\frac{5}{9} - 2\frac{3}{9} = 2\frac{2}{9}$ Ans. $2\frac{2}{9}$ meters of tape

40 Subtraction
Mixed Numbers: Part Five ① p.41

1 $2\frac{7}{5}$, $1\frac{3}{5}$

2 (1) $3\frac{4}{3}$, $2\frac{2}{3}$ (2) $1\frac{6}{4}$, $\frac{3}{4}$ (3) $1\frac{3}{7}$ (4) $\frac{5}{6}$

3 $4\frac{1}{3} - 1\frac{2}{3} = 3\frac{4}{3} - 1\frac{2}{3}$

$= 2\frac{2}{3}$ Ans. $2\frac{2}{3}$ quarts

41 Subtraction
Mixed Numbers: Part Five ② p.42

1 (1) $4\frac{10}{6}$, $1\frac{5}{6}$ (2) $2\frac{11}{9}$, $\frac{7}{9}$

2 (1) $2\frac{4}{7}$ (2) $1\frac{7}{8}$ (3) $3\frac{3}{5}$ (4) $\frac{2}{3}$

3 $3\frac{2}{4} - 2\frac{3}{4} = 2\frac{6}{4} - 2\frac{3}{4}$

$= \frac{3}{4}$ Ans. $\frac{3}{4}$ of a yard

42 Subtraction
Whole Number − Proper Fraction ① p.43

1 $1\frac{5}{5}$, $1\frac{2}{5}$

2 (1) $\frac{8}{8}$, $\frac{5}{8}$ (2) $1\frac{4}{4}$, $1\frac{3}{4}$ (3) $\frac{1}{5}$ (4) $1\frac{5}{6}$

3 $3 - \frac{1}{4} = 2\frac{4}{4} - \frac{1}{4}$

$= 2\frac{3}{4}$ Ans. $2\frac{3}{4}$ crates

43 Subtraction
Whole Number − Proper Fraction ② p.44

1 (1) $2\frac{3}{3}$, $2\frac{2}{3}$ (2) $3\frac{5}{5}$, $3\frac{3}{5}$

2 (1) $2\frac{7}{7}$, $2\frac{4}{7}$ (2) $2\frac{1}{3}$ (3) $3\frac{3}{10}$ (4) $3\frac{5}{8}$

3 $3 - \frac{7}{10} = 2\frac{10}{10} - \frac{7}{10}$

$= 2\frac{3}{10}$ Ans. $2\frac{3}{10}$ pies

44 Subtraction
Whole Number − Proper Fraction ③ p.45

1 (1) $\frac{2}{9}$ (3) $1\frac{9}{10}$ (5) $3\frac{1}{3}$

(2) $1\frac{1}{4}$ (4) $2\frac{3}{8}$ (6) $2\frac{5}{6}$

2 $1 - \frac{3}{8} = \frac{8}{8} - \frac{3}{8}$

$= \frac{5}{8}$ Ans. $\frac{5}{8}$ of the pizza

45 Subtraction
Whole Number − Mixed Number ① p.46

1 $2\dfrac{5}{5}$, $1\dfrac{3}{5}$

2 (1) $1\dfrac{7}{7}$, $\dfrac{4}{7}$ (2) $2\dfrac{4}{4}$, $1\dfrac{1}{4}$ (3) $\dfrac{1}{6}$ (4) $1\dfrac{5}{9}$

3 $3 - 1\dfrac{3}{4} = 2\dfrac{4}{4} - 1\dfrac{3}{4}$

$\qquad\qquad = 1\dfrac{1}{4}$　Ans. $1\dfrac{1}{4}$ gallons

46 Subtraction
Whole Number − Mixed Number ② p.47

1 (1) $3\dfrac{4}{4}$, $2\dfrac{3}{4}$ (2) $4\dfrac{8}{8}$, $2\dfrac{5}{8}$

2 (1) $2\dfrac{6}{6}$, $1\dfrac{5}{6}$ (2) $1\dfrac{3}{10}$ (3) $2\dfrac{5}{7}$ (4) $3\dfrac{1}{5}$

3 $3 - 2\dfrac{5}{9} = 2\dfrac{9}{9} - 2\dfrac{5}{9}$

$\qquad\qquad = \dfrac{4}{9}$　Ans. $\dfrac{4}{9}$ of a yard

47 Subtraction
Whole Number − Mixed Number ③ p.48

1 (1) $\dfrac{7}{8}$ (3) $1\dfrac{4}{9}$ (5) $3\dfrac{7}{10}$

(2) $2\dfrac{2}{3}$ (4) $\dfrac{6}{7}$ (6) $2\dfrac{1}{4}$

2 $3 - 1\dfrac{1}{6} = 2\dfrac{6}{6} - 1\dfrac{1}{6}$

$\qquad\qquad = 1\dfrac{5}{6}$　Ans. $1\dfrac{5}{6}$ pounds of flour

48 Subtraction
Mixed p.49

1 (1) $\dfrac{1}{6}$ (3) $\dfrac{9}{10}$ (5) $1\dfrac{7}{9}$

(2) $1\dfrac{2}{5}$ (4) $1\dfrac{5}{7}$ (6) $2\dfrac{1}{4}$

2 $1\dfrac{2}{4} - \dfrac{3}{4} = \dfrac{6}{4} - \dfrac{3}{4}$

$\qquad\qquad = \dfrac{3}{4}$　Ans. $\dfrac{3}{4}$ of a mile

49 Introduction
Review ① p.50

1 (1) $<$　(2) $>$　(3) $<$

2 (1) A : 0.5　B : 1.8　C : 2.6

(2) A : 10.2　B : 11.4　C : 12.6

50 Introduction
Review ② p.51

1 (1) $<$　(2) $>$　(3) $=$

2 (1) A : 0.05　B : 0.18　C : 0.26

(2) A : 2.92　B : 3.01　C : 3.19

51 Addition
Up to Tenths Place ① p.52

1 (1) 1.8　(2) 2.8

2 (1) 2.8　(3) 7.6　(5) 9.4

(2) 3.8　(4) 0.9　(6) 3.1

3 $3.3 + 0.5 = 3.8$　Ans. 3.8 grams

52 Addition
Up to Tenths Place ② p.53

1 (1) 1.9　(2) 4.1

2 (1) 2.2　(3) 2.9　(5) 1.5

(2) 8.9　(4) 3.9　(6) 5.2

3 $0.6 + 1.5 = 2.1$　Ans. 2.1 feet of ribbon

53 Addition
Up to Tenths Place ③ p.54

1 (1) 3.7　(2) 1.3　(3) 5.5　(4) 5.2

2 (1) 1.3　(3) 3.1　(5) 4.1

(2) 3.7　(4) 4.2　(6) 2.4

3 $1.5 + 0.8 = 2.3$　Ans. 2.3 oz

54 Addition
Up to Hundredths Place: Part One ① p.55

1 (1) 0.82 (2) 0.61

2 (1) 0.56 (3) 0.82 (5) 0.73

(2) 0.95 (4) 0.87 (6) 0.61

3 0.37 + 0.45 = 0.82   Ans. 0.82 miles

55 Addition
Up to Hundredths Place: Part One ② p.56

1 (1) 1.11 (2) 1.05 (3) 0.93

2 (1) 1.55 (3) 0.92 (5) 1.09

(2) 1.03 (4) 0.32 (6) 1.31

3 0.57 + 0.86 = 1.43   Ans. 1.43 cm

56 Addition
Up to Hundredths Place: Part One ③ p.57

1 (1) 0.86 (4) 1.54 (7) 1.18

(2) 1.02 (5) 0.83 (8) 1.03

(3) 0.62 (6) 1.25 (9) 0.82

2 0.41 + 0.95 = 1.36   Ans. 1.36 kilograms

57 Addition
Up to Hundredths Place: Part Two ① p.58

1 (1) 4.81 (2) 3.58

2 (1) 7.38 (3) 6.97 (5) 6.19

(2) 8.59 (4) 4.26 (6) 7.51

3 2.47 + 6.12 = 8.59   Ans. 8.59 km²

58 Addition
Up to Hundredths Place: Part Two ② p.59

1 (1) 7.81 (2) 2.49 (3) 8.73

2 (1) 8.11 (3) 7.58 (5) 6.91

(2) 3.21 (4) 7.22 (6) 9.06

3 1.28 + 3.53 = 4.81   Ans. 4.81 gallons

59 Addition
Up to Hundredths Place: Part Two ③ p.60

1 (1) 3.26 (4) 8.01 (7) 8.19

(2) 5.09 (5) 8.26 (8) 9.04

(3) 7.77 (6) 7.71 (9) 8.24

2 1.36 + 4.15 = 5.51   Ans. 5.51 pounds

60 Addition
Up to Thousandths Place: Part One ① p.61

1 (1) 0.852 (2) 0.661

2 (1) 0.873 (3) 0.434 (5) 0.806

(2) 0.679 (4) 0.919 (6) 0.825

3 0.176 + 0.258 = 0.434   Ans. 0.434 tons

61 Addition
Up to Thousandths Place: Part One ② p.62

1 (1) 0.744 (2) 0.612 (3) 0.661

2 (1) 0.664 (3) 0.191 (5) 0.919

(2) 0.825 (4) 0.401 (6) 0.731

3 0.465 + 0.387 = 0.852   Ans. 0.825 liters of water

62 Addition
Up to Thousandths Place: Part One ③ p.63

1 (1) 0.798 (4) 0.551 (7) 0.637

(2) 0.796 (5) 0.246 (8) 0.903

(3) 0.503 (6) 0.851 (9) 0.802

2 0.406 + 0.597 = 1.003   Ans. 1.003 gallons

63 Addition
Up to Thousandths Place: Part Two ① p.64

1 (1) 5.397 (2) 5.707

2 (1) 5.851 (3) 5.804 (5) 7.232

(2) 6.661 (4) 8.921 (6) 7.626

3 4.193 + 2.468 = 6.661   Ans. 6.661 pounds

64 Addition
Up to Thousandths Place: Part Two ② p.65

1 (1) 10.123 (2) 7.911 (3) 10.094

2 (1) 5.889 (3) 8.602 (5) 10.041

(2) 8.885 (4) 10.651 (6) 10.065

3 1.485＋3.912＝5.397 Ans. 5.397 inches

65 Addition
Up to Thousandths Place: Part Two ③ p.66

1 (1) 6.921 (4) 8.717 (7) 10.316

(2) 8.668 (5) 8.802 (8) 10.005

(3) 4.065 (6) 8.172 (9) 10.008

2 3.259＋4.743＝8.002 Ans. 8.002 grams

66 Addition
The Last Digit Becomes 0 ① p.67

1 (1) 6.2 (2) 6

2 (1) 2.8 (3) 8.5 (5) 9

(2) 4.7 (4) 9 (6) 10

3 4.52＋3.98＝8.5 Ans. 8.5 pounds

67 Addition
The Last Digit Becomes 0 ② p.68

1 (1) 14 (2) 20 (3) 0.8

2 (1) 4 (3) 0.8 (5) 0.1

(2) 15 (4) 0.6 (6) 0.9

3 0.96＋5.04＝6 Ans. 6 kilometers

68 Addition
The Last Digit Becomes 0 ③ p.69

1 (1) 4.5 (4) 10 (7) 0.3

(2) 9.9 (5) 13 (8) 0.7

(3) 8 (6) 15 (9) 0.9

2 0.35＋1.25＝1.6 Ans. 1.6 yards

69 Addition
Different Digits: Part One ① p.70

1 (1) 3.13 (2) 10.52

2 (1) 2.82 (3) 7.97 (5) 10.12

(2) 3.13 (4) 8.47 (6) 11.58

3 2.63＋0.5＝3.13 Ans. 3.13 kilograms

70 Addition
Different Digits: Part One ② p.71

1 (1) 3.652 (2) 6.315 (3) 2.004

2 (1) 7.714 (3) 8.504 (5) 2.028

(2) 5.802 (4) 6.089 (6) 2.003

3 4.225＋4.13＝8.355 Ans. 8.355 miles

71 Addition
Different Digits: Part One ③ p.72

1 (1) 6.51 (4) 10.84 (7) 8.908

(2) 9.59 (5) 10.02 (8) 9.153

(3) 5.37 (6) 8.491 (9) 8.083

2 1.35＋0.8＝2.15 Ans. 2.15 oz

72 Addition
Different Digits: Part Two ① p.73

1 (1) 5.22 (2) 7.42

2 (1) 6.85 (3) 5.22 (5) 9.21

(2) 1.98 (4) 9.78 (6) 10.55

3 1.3＋3.92＝5.22 Ans. 5.22 kilometers

73 Addition
Different Digits: Part Two ② p.74

1 (1) 4.574 (2) 4.035 (3) 5.303

2 (1) 3.539 (3) 7.204 (5) 8.187

(2) 7.821 (4) 5.801 (6) 5.023

3 4.5 + 3.425 = 7.925 Ans. 7.925 oz

74 Addition
Different Digits: Part Two ③ p.75

1 (1) 6.44 (4) 9.98 (7) 9.704

(2) 3.11 (5) 10.33 (8) 8.859

(3) 9.17 (6) 5.878 (9) 7.046

2 0.4 + 1.75 = 2.15 Ans. 2.15 yards

75 Addition
Mixed p.76

1 (1) 5.4 (4) 6.21 (7) 5

(2) 4.02 (5) 0.962 (8) 8.27

(3) 1.02 (6) 7.001 (9) 5.436

2 2.5 + 3.86 = 6.36 Ans. 6.36 miles

76 Subtraction
Up to Tenths Place ① p.77

1 (1) 1.2 (2) 3.1

2 (1) 0.7 (3) 2.1 (5) 5.5

(2) 1.5 (4) 2.1 (6) 1.4

3 2.5 − 0.4 = 2.1 Ans. 2.1 pints

77 Subtraction
Up to Tenths Place ② p.78

1 (1) 0.5 (2) 1.9

2 (1) 0.3 (3) 1.9 (5) 2.9

(2) 3.3 (4) 2.1 (6) 3.4

3 5.6 − 0.8 = 4.8 Ans. 4.8 gallons

78 Subtraction
Up to Tenths Place ③ p.79

1 (1) 6.1 (2) 3.8 (3) 0.8 (4) 3.4

2 (1) 1.3 (3) 4.6 (5) 0.1

(2) 1.5 (4) 0.4 (6) 8.8

3 1.2 − 0.9 = 0.3 Ans. 0.3 feet

79 Subtraction
Up to Hundredths Place: Part One ① p.80

1 (1) 1.28 (2) 2.32

2 (1) 2.12 (3) 3.01 (5) 1.28

(2) 2.51 (4) 7.09 (6) 9.69

3 3.46 − 2.18 = 1.28 Ans. 1.28 cm

80 Subtraction
Up to Hundredths Place: Part One ② p.81

1 (1) 7.27 (2) 13.31 (3) 14.31

2 (1) 10.63 (3) 8.22 (5) 15.65

(2) 15.67 (4) 18.25 (6) 12.19

3 12.43 − 5.16 = 7.27 Ans. 7.27 grams

81 Subtraction Up to Hundredths Place: Part One ③ p.82

1 (1) 5.32　(4) 8.69　(7) 16.89
(2) 4.09　(5) 10.01　(8) 20.47
(3) 3.06　(6) 6.34　(9) 2.63

2 5.26−1.45=3.81　Ans. 3.81 inches

82 Subtraction Up to Hundredths Place: Part Two ① p.83

1 (1) 0.28　(2) 0.64

2 (1) 0.83　(3) 0.15　(5) 0.87
(2) 0.73　(4) 0.17　(6) 0.99

3 1.56−0.92=0.64　Ans. 0.64 liters

83 Subtraction Up to Hundredths Place: Part Two ② p.84

1 (1) 0.99　(2) 0.75　(3) 0.29

2 (1) 0.08　(3) 0.83　(5) 0.54
(2) 0.99　(4) 0.73　(6) 0.89

3 9.53−8.56=0.97　Ans. 0.97 oz

84 Subtraction Up to Hundredths Place: Part Two ③ p.85

1 (1) 0.91　(4) 0.62　(7) 0.79
(2) 0.21　(5) 0.28　(8) 0.92
(3) 0.08　(6) 0.83　(9) 0.71

2 2.74−2.56=0.18　Ans. 0.18 pounds

85 Subtraction Up to Thousandths Place: Part One ① p.86

1 (1) 4.088　(2) 1.295

2 (1) 4.851　(3) 2.912　(5) 2.251
(2) 2.611　(4) 4.052　(6) 2.809

3 3.152−0.541=2.611　Ans. 2.611 miles

86 Subtraction Up to Thousandths Place: Part One ② p.87

1 (1) 3.768　(2) 1.918　(3) 2.401

2 (1) 1.484　(3) 2.263　(5) 4.374
(2) 5.724　(4) 1.008　(6) 1.829

3 9.103−4.098=5.005　Ans. 5.005 kilograms

87 Subtraction Up to Thousandths Place: Part One ③ p.88

1 (1) 1.833　(4) 4.739　(7) 2.071
(2) 4.068　(5) 4.677　(8) 1.131
(3) 3.648　(6) 2.927　(9) 6.659

2 8.209−4.163=4.046　Ans. 4.046 liters

88 Subtraction Up to Thousandths Place: Part Two ① p.89

1 (1) 0.621　(2) 0.804

2 (1) 0.815　(3) 0.621　(5) 0.864
(2) 0.198　(4) 0.586　(6) 0.922

3 5.763−5.142=0.621　Ans. 0.621 meters

89 Subtraction Up to Thousandths Place: Part Two ② p.90

1 (1) 0.241　(2) 0.274　(3) 0.893

2 (1) 0.302　(3) 0.337　(5) 0.649
(2) 0.143　(4) 0.914　(6) 0.196

3 4.705−3.762=0.943　Ans. 0.943 inches

90 Subtraction Up to Thousandths Place: Part Two ③ p.91

1 (1) 0.176　(4) 0.433　(7) 0.731
(2) 0.152　(5) 0.373　(8) 0.259
(3) 0.219　(6) 0.286　(9) 0.421

2 6.251−5.634=0.617　Ans. 0.617 pounds

91 Subtraction
The Last Digit Becomes 0 ① p.92

1 (1) 1.4 (2) 4

2 (1) 3.1 (3) 8   (5) 10

(2) 1.4 (4) 12 (6) 6

3 4.34 − 2.94 = 1.4   Ans. 1.4 yards

92 Subtraction
The Last Digit Becomes 0 ② p.93

1 (1) 5.6 (2) 1.43 (3) 0.07

2 (1) 1.5 (3) 2.11 (5) 0.06

(2) 10 (4) 2.19 (6) 0.09

3 12.64 − 8.64 = 4   Ans. 4 cm

93 Subtraction
The Last Digit Becomes 0 ③ p.94

1 (1) 1.1 (4) 11.9 (7) 4.7

(2) 10 (5) 3.2 (8) 2.8

(3) 17 (6) 6.78 (9) 6

2 2.35 − 0.75 = 1.6   Ans. 1.6 kilograms

94 Subtraction
Different Digits: Part One ① p.95

1 (1) 2.34 (2) 3.33

2 (1) 1.43 (3) 2.34 (5) 1.96

(2) 2.13 (4) 3.81 (6) 1.68

3 8.24 − 5.9 = 2.34   Ans. 2.34 pounds

95 Subtraction
Different Digits: Part One ② p.96

1 (1) 0.183 (2) 3.881 (3) 5.39

2 (1) 0.142 (3) 4.347 (5) 6.23

(2) 0.188 (4) 4.254 (6) 10.42

3 12.09 − 6.7 = 5.39   Ans. 5.39 oz

96 Subtraction
Different Digits: Part One ③ p.97

1 (1) 2.39 (4) 0.331 (7) 2.387

(2) 3.93 (5) 0.467 (8) 6.52

(3) 1.82 (6) 4.504 (9) 5.75

2 3.52 − 1.6 = 1.92   Ans. 1.92 pounds

97 Subtraction
Different Digits: Part Two ① p.98

1 (1) 1.64 (2) 2.58

2 (1) 1.36 (3) 14.18 (5) 3.52

(2) 2.67 (4) 3.84 (6) 15.37

3 6.1 − 3.43 = 2.67   Ans. 2.67 feet

98 Subtraction
Different Digits: Part Two ② p.99

1 (1) 0.825 (2) 1.747 (3) 0.117

2 (1) 1.139 (3) 4.054 (5) 0.731

(2) 4.936 (4) 7.545 (6) 1.884

3 7 − 3.315 = 3.685   Ans. 3.685 quarts

99 Subtraction
Different Digits: Part Two ③ p.100

1 (1) 3.08 (4) 4.815 (7) 2.926

(2) 17.17 (5) 2.049 (8) 0.564

(3) 11.32 (6) 6.372 (9) 1.732

2 3.2 − 0.89 = 2.31   Ans. 2.31 liters

100 Subtraction
Mixed p.101

1 (1) 2.5 (4) 0.29 (7) 5.21

(2) 13.21 (5) 2.439 (8) 1.77

(3) 4.57 (6) 0.921 (9) 0.472

2 4 − 2.45 = 1.55   Ans. 1.55 feet